Journey
to English

CARINA GUINAME SHIROMA
MAURICIO SHIROMA

3

© Text: Carina Guiname Shiroma and Mauricio Shiroma
© Design and illustration: Macmillan do Brasil 2012

Executive managing editor: Wilma Moura
Editors: Andréa Vidal and Isabel Lacombe
Assistant editors: Amanda Lenharo di Santis and Ana Carolina de Castro Gasonato
Teacher's guide collaborator: Vitor Sugita
Language consultant: Robert C. Garner
Proofreader: Maria Cecilia Jorgewich Skaf
Translators: Amini Rassoul, Anthony Doyle, and Maria Cecilia Jorgewich Skaf
Permissions coordinator: Fernando Santos
Minidictionary editor: Ana Carolina de Castro Gasonato

Concept design and page make-up: Maps World Produções Gráficas
Design editor: Jorge Okura
Cover concept and design: Alexandre Tallarico
Concept design: Alexandre Tallarico and Carolina de Oliveira
Page make-up: Alexandre Tallarico, Carolina de Oliveira, and Vivian Trevizan
Proofreader: Ana Cristina Mendes Perfetti

Illustrator: Sidney Meireles (Giz de Cera)

Audio recording, mixing, and mastering: Maximal Studio
DVD illustrations, animations, infographs, software, and website: Maximal Studio

Dados Internacionais de Catalogação na Publicação (CIP)
(Câmara Brasileira do Livro, SP, Brasil)

Shiroma, Carina Guiname
  Journey to English / Carina Guiname Shiroma, Mauricio Shiroma. -- 1. ed. -- São Paulo : Macmillan, 2012.

  ISBN 978-85-7418-862-1 (v. 1, student`s book)
  ISBN 978-85-7418-864-5 (v. 2, student`s book)
  ISBN 978-85-7418-866-9 (v. 3, student`s book)
  ISBN 978-85-7418-868-3 (v. 4, student`s book)

  1. Inglês (Ensino fundamental) I. Shiroma, Mauricio. II. Título.

12-06867   CDD-372.652

Índices para catálogo sistemático:
1. Inglês : Ensino fundamental 372.652

Macmillan do Brasil
Rua José Félix de Oliveira, 383 – Granja Viana
06708-645 – Cotia – SP – Brasil
www.macmillan.com.br
elt@macmillan.com.br

Caro aluno,

Você já deve ter ouvido que "toda jornada começa com o primeiro passo", não é? Pois o primeiro passo da nossa jornada foi dado há muito tempo, quando nós tínhamos a sua idade e começamos a estudar inglês.

Quando embarcamos nessa viagem que é aprender uma nova língua, tínhamos os sonhos de todos os viajantes: visitar lugares distantes, conhecer pessoas incríveis, entender o que o mundo fala e conseguir nos comunicar com ele. Porém, naquela época, antes das maravilhas e facilidades tecnológicas que você conhece hoje, a jornada era bastante difícil: havia muitos obstáculos e poucos atalhos. As dificuldades deixavam a jornada mais lenta, mas nem por isso menos interessante.

O segredo de todo bom viajante é saber se adaptar ao ritmo que cada trecho impõe. Em alguns trechos, viajamos na velocidade da luz; em outros, nos deixamos levar pela maré calma. Além disso, como em toda jornada, havia muitos caminhos à frente, e saber escolher o melhor deles fazia parte do desafio de chegar. Apesar de o destino ter sido o objetivo final da jornada, saber aproveitar as delícias do percurso foi, sem dúvida, o que mais nos encantou.

"Mas eles chegaram aonde?", você deve estar se perguntando.

Chegamos aqui, agora. E já podemos traçar o caminho para você, que está dando aquele primeiro passo rumo à mesma jornada de aprender uma língua.

Este livro é um mapa da jornada para você; use-o, transforme-o, descubra novos caminhos e possibilidades. Compartilhe as experiências com outros viajantes e divirta-se sempre.

Que você faça uma excelente viagem!

Carina e Mauricio

Know your book

Unit sections

Opening
The pictures in the opening pages of each unit are intended to stimulate impressions, feelings, and reactions, and lead to reflection on the theme.

Itinerary
Itinerary introduces the contents explored in each unit. This section allows you to evaluate what you already know and get ready / prepare yourself for what you will learn.

This icon indicates activities that focus on the characteristics of the text genre studied.

Reading
In the reading activities, you analyze and interpret different texts and learn strategies to make reading easier and more enjoyable. This section provides not only basic reading comprehension tasks, but also topics for reflection and discussion which will contribute to your education as a critical citizen.

Your Take
In these activities, you give your opinion and share ideas with classmates about the topics explored in the unit.

Listening

In this section, you listen to a great variety of oral genres. The activities use strategies that make listening easier.

SKIM — This icon indicates that the activity provides practice in understanding the gist of the text.

SCAN — This icon indicates that the activity practices comprehension of specific and detailed information from the text.

Speaking

In this section you learn how to gradually communicate in English in daily situations through conversation activities – from the most simple, such as making suggestions, to the most complex, such as making a speech in class.

Vocabulary

In this section, you learn the meaning and pronunciation of words and expressions, which will expand your possibilities of communication in English. The section also helps you organize your knowledge.

Pronunciation

Pronunciation works as a support for the speaking and oral comprehension activities. This section contains dialogs, visual aids, and phonetic symbols to make you feel more confident and become more efficient in oral communication.

Grammar

In this section, you are exposed to grammar within a communicative context to facilitate understanding. The activities help you analyze the patterns of language and draw conclusions about its rules. With this material, you learn how to use grammar both to produce and to understand oral and written texts.

Road to Success

This section helps develop learner autonomy in general by providing several strategies, techniques, and tips for you to succeed in learning English.

Writing

Writing is seen as a process. Here you learn to use different resources to plan, outline, revise, and edit so you can write with autonomy. The genres you will produce will be shared with different audiences and published in different media.

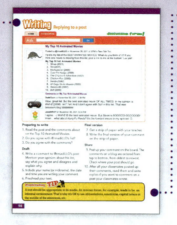

Proofreading Tip

These boxes provide practical production, revision, and editing tips for you to gradually achieve autonomy in the writing process.

Reflect

In this section, you think over the activities and texts in order to develop a critical sense. It encourages your personal engagement as a citizen.

Crossroads

Here you use English to learn, expand, or review contents from other school subjects.

This icon indicates that the question(s) can only be answered by using logical deduction along with the information in the text.

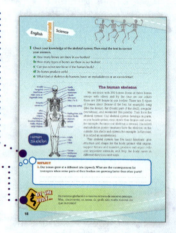

By the Way

This section provides comments about language and culture to expand and contextualize the different topics in the unit.

This icon tells you that there is an activity on the DVD-ROM. When you see this symbol, go to page 166 and find the objectives, description, and tips to do the activity.

Extras

Looking Back

At the end of each unit, this self-evaluation tool will help you develop autonomy in learning English. Here you reflect on whether you have reached the goals established or still need more revision. You will also find suggestions for further study, such as websites, other resources in this book, and other useful titles.

Stopover

Every two units, you stop to review the content with fun and relaxing activities. This section will allow you to evaluate yourself and improve your knowledge in an enjoyable way.

6

Review
Every four units, you have a systematic, comprehensive review. You can test your knowledge and judge whether you need to practice more or not.

Grammar Reference
All the knowledge built in class is systematized in this section. It works as reference to study and review grammar.

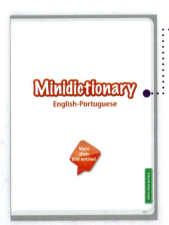

Minidictionary
This is a bilingual dictionary with all the key words introduced in each book. Organized in alphabetical order, it provides the translation of the word or expression, the phonetic transcription, the word frequency, the word class, and examples of use.

Project
Every two units there is a project involving research, planning, preparation, and presentation. It is an opportunity to put English into practice in real contexts both inside and outside of school.

Extra Reading
Every two units, there is an extra text to develop reading skills. The texts are authentic and accompanied by activities that provide more practice for you to feel comfortable when reading.

A ⇄ B
For some conversation practices, there are special activities that can only be done with the exchange of information between two students. The section simulates a situation that is common in our daily speech – the search for information.

7

Contents

In all shapes and colors page 12

- 14 **Reading** Olympic sports and body types
- 16 **Vocabulary** Physical appearance
- 18 **Crossroads** Science: skeletal system
- 19 **Listening** A physical evaluation
- 20 **Writing** Medical evaluation form
- 21 **Grammar** To be vs. other verbs
- 23 **Pronunciation** Stop sounds
- 23 **Speaking** Show and tell
- 23 **Road to Success** At your own pace

I'm going through changes page 24

- 26 **Reading** Infographic
- 28 **Vocabulary** Puberty issues
- 29 **Speaking** Giving advice
- 30 **Listening** News report about puberty
- 31 **Grammar** Comparative form
- 33 **Crossroads** Physical education: coordination
- 34 **Pronunciation** You say tomato, I say "tomahto".
- 34 **Road to Success** Dealing with puberty
- 35 **Writing** A message in an internet forum

| 36 Stopover – Units 1&2 | 38 Extra Reading 1 | 40 Project 1 |

Technology page 42

- 44 **Reading** Electronics advertisement
- 46 **Vocabulary** Technology problems
- 48 **Grammar** Used to
- 49 **Pronunciation** Used to
- 50 **Speaking** Expressing doubt and disbelief
- 51 **Crossroads** Math: bits and bytes
- 52 **Road to Success** Using technology to learn English
- 52 **Listening** Calling a call center
- 53 **Writing** Online customer support form

Almanac mania page 54

- 56 **Reading** The 90s in an almanac
- 58 **Vocabulary** Almanac topics
- 60 **Grammar** Verb to be – past
- 61 **Pronunciation** Reduction of was + subject pronoun
- 62 **Listening** A TV game show
- 63 **Crossroads** History of Brazil: presidents
- 64 **Road to Success** My English was, my English is
- 64 **Speaking** Agreeing and disagreeing
- 65 **Writing** A class almanac

| 66 Stopover – Units 3&4 | 70 Project 2 | 74 Review – Units 1 to 4 |
| 68 Extra Reading 2 | 72 Looking Back at Units 1 to 4 | |

8

Everyday mythology page 76

- 78 **Reading** Quiz: How much do you know about the influence of mythology in our everyday life?
- 81 **Road to Success** Language learning myths
- 82 **Vocabulary** Talking about personality
- 83 **Grammar** There to be – past
- 84 **Crossroads** Language: etymology
- 85 **Pronunciation** Pronunciation in a dictionary
- 85 **Listening** Storytelling
- 86 **Speaking** Asking for clarification
- 87 **Writing** Movie review

The young and talented page 88

- 90 **Reading** A DVD blurb
- 92 **Vocabulary** Professions
- 94 **Crossroads** Social sciences: EQ
- 95 **Speaking** Showing surprise
- 95 **Pronunciation** Syllables & rhythm
- 96 **Grammar** Superlative form
- 98 **Writing** Replying to a post
- 99 **Listening** A newscast

100 **Stopover** – Units 5&6   102 **Extra Reading 3**   104 **Project 3**

Black Power page 106

- 108 **Reading** Black Power: much more than a haircut
- 110 **Vocabulary** Clothes
- 112 **Speaking** Giving and responding to compliments
- 113 **Grammar** Relative pronouns – who, which, that
- 114 **Crossroads** Music: African instruments
- 114 **Road to Success** Learning English with music
- 115 **Pronunciation** The sounds of the letter i
- 115 **Listening** An oral presentation
- 116 **Writing & Speaking** A speech about an African-Brazilian I admire

Homemade gifts page 118

- 120 **Reading** A homemade gift
- 121 **Vocabulary** Handcraft
- 123 **Crossroads** Geography: flags and gifts traditions around the world
- 125 **Listening** Secret Santa
- 126 **Pronunciation** The sound of the letter u
- 126 **Speaking** Giving and accepting gifts
- 127 **Grammar** Some / any – countable vs uncountable
- 128 **Road to Success** A gift to yourself
- 129 **Writing** A gift card

130 **Stopover** – Units 7&8   134 **Project 4**   138 **Review** – Units 5 to 8
132 **Extra Reading 4**   136 **Looking Back at Units 5 to 8**

EXTRAS

- 140 **Grammar Reference**
- 148 **A⇄B**
- 151 **Minidictionary**
- 164 **Sites**
- 165 **Bibliography**
- 166 **DVD-ROM info**

9

Name: ....

School: ....

School address: ....

....

City: ....

State: ....

ZIP code: ....

School telephone number: ....

School email: ....

English teacher: ....

Class schedule					
Monday	Tuesday	Wednesday	Thursday	Friday	Saturday

Test agenda					
January	February	March	April	May	June
July	August	September	October	November	December

Classroom Language

UNIT 1
In all shapes and colors

ITINERARY

In this unit, you will develop the following competences:
- reading a sports webpage to get general and specific information about Olympic sports and body types;
- learning words and expressions to describe physical appearance;
- reading a text to learn more about the human skeleton;
- listening to a conversation to get general and specific information about a physical evaluation;
- completing a medical evaluation form with personal information;
- contrasting the verb *to be* and other verbs to talk about physical appearance and sports;
- practicing the stop sounds to learn the pronunciation of some words in this unit;
- presenting a show and introducing someone you admire to your classmates;
- reflecting on your pace of learning to be more confident in your studies..

Reading Olympic sports and body types

1 Write the name of the sports under the correct pictures.

discus throw ▪ rhythmic ▪ shot put ▪ sprint ▪ triathlon ▪ weightlifting ▪ wrestling

a t ....

b r .... gymnastics.

c s ....

d d ....

e w ....

f w ....

g s ....

h a .... gymnastics

2 Look at the text on the next page and answer the questions. GENRE

a Where can you find a text like this?

....

b Where is the website from?

◯ USA.   ◯ Australia.   ◯ South Africa.   ◯ England.

c How do you know the origin of the website?

....

d The website is a...

◯ sports magazine.   ◯ daily newspaper.   ◯ fashion blog.

e How do you know the answer to **item d**?

....

....

....

YOUR TAKE

Do you think we should choose the sport we want to practice based on our body types?

....

AmeliaBurton.com.au
Health and Fitness Coach

home | about | advertise | contribute | training

Search

inspiration • motivation • education

What body type are you?

What is your body shape? Would you be best suited as a marathon runner, 100m sprinter, or a shot putter?

Ectomorph: These are lean, lightweight athletes who are good at distance sports that need muscle resistance.
- thin.
- lightly muscled.
- has problems gaining weight.
- muscle growth takes longer.
- has fast metabolism.

Olympic Sports choices: marathon running, triathlon, rhythmic gymnastics, basketball, soccer.

Endomorph: These are heavier athletes who naturally carry more body fat and do best in sports that need power and body weight force.
- round and soft shape.
- arms and legs of the extreme endomorph are usually short in length.
- body has a high waist.
- weight loss is difficult.
- gains muscle easily.

Olympic Sports choices: wrestling, shot put, discus throw, weightlifting.

Mesomorph: These are naturally muscular athletes with low body fat and good at sports that need strength and power.
- wider shoulders, narrow and low waist.
- arms and legs are developed.
- athletic.
- hard, muscular body.
- gains or loses weight easily.

Olympic Sports choices: boxing (heavy weight), cycling (sprint distances), athletic sprint events (100m is the best example), artistic gymnastics.

Although some people are clearly one of the above body types, most of us are a mix. For example, a lot of endomorphs also have the muscular shape of a mesomorph (an endo-mesomorph mix).
Everyone is genetically predisposed to being a certain body type, but with training, environmental influences, and diet, you can change what you are genetically appropriate to do. But if you are an ectomorph and you want to become a sumo wrestler, good luck!

Disclaimer: The information within this website is intended as reference only and not as medical or professional advice. Never begin a dietary or exercise program without first consulting with a qualified healthcare professional.

Adapted from AmeliaBurton.com.au

Unit 1 – In all shapes and colors

3 Read the text again and answer T (true) or F (false).

a ◯ It's not easy for ectomorphs to gain weight.
b ◯ Ectomorphs are good at sports that need power and body weight force.
c ◯ It's difficult for endomorphs to lose weight.
d ◯ Artistic gymnastics is a good sport for mesomorphs.
e ◯ It is common for people to be a mix of the body types.

4 Match the body type to the sport according to the text.

cycling   high jumping   hammer throw

◯ endomorph
◯ mesomorph
◯ ectomorph

5 The author finishes the article saying "Good luck!". Who is the author wishing good luck to?

◯ Endomorphs.   ◯ Mesomorphs.   ◯ Ectomorphs.

6 Why does the author wish good luck? INFER

....
....

Vocabulary   Physical appearance

1 Read and listen to the physical descriptions below. Underline the adjectives used for describing physical appearance. 🎧 3

Arturo is a jockey. He is slim and short. He is light-skinned, and he has short black hair and black eyes.

Kwasi is a marathon runner. He is dark-skinned, skinny, and average height. He has short black hair.

Massao is a sumo wrestler. He is tall and fat. He has straight black hair.

Grigori is tall and chubby, but athletic. He has short brown hair and brown eyes.

16

2 Write the adjectives from activity 1 in the correct category. Also include the words below in the correct column.

wavy and red

long and blond

blue

short and curly

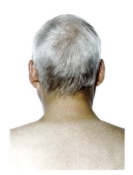
gray

Height	Build	Hair style	Hair color	Complexion	Eyes

3 Use the adjectives of description to talk about the people below.

He **is** (height, build, complexion).
He **has** (hair style, hair color, eyes).

a  b  c  d  e  f

4 What about you? How do you describe yourself?

....

....

Unit 1 – In all shapes and colors

17

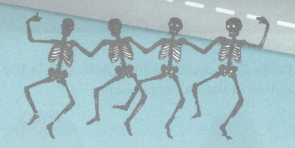

English Crossroads **Science**

1. Check your knowledge of the skeletal system. Then read the text to correct your answers.

   a How many bones are there in our bodies? ....
   b How many types of bones are there in our bodies? ....
   c Can you name one bone of the human body? ....
   d Do bones produce cells? ....
   e What kind of skeleton do humans have: an endoskeleton or an exoskeleton?
   ....

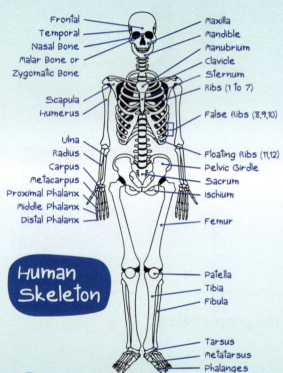

The human skeleton

We are born with 300 bones. Some of these bones merge with others and by the time we are adults, there are 206 bones in our bodies. There are 5 types of bones: short (bones of the foot, for example), long (like the femur), flat (frontal part of the skull), irregular (vertebrae), and sesamoid (the patella). They form the skeletal system. Our skeletal system develops in parts, so our heads grow more slowly than fingers and arms, for example. Because our skeleton is internal, it is called endoskeleton. (Some creatures have the skeleton on the outside, like shells and oysters, for example. In this case, it is called an exoskeleton.)

This skeletal system has five basic functions: to give structure and shape for the body, to protect vital organs, to support tissues and muscles, to produce and repair cells and important minerals, and to help the body move in different directions and ways.

REFLECT

1. Our bones grow at a different rate (speed). What are the consequences for teenagers when some parts of their bodies are growing faster than other parts?

   ....
   ....

Humans and giraffes have the same number of bones in their necks. But the bones in a giraffe are bigger.

18

Listening — A physical evaluation

1 Listen and choose the photo that illustrates the dialog. SKIM

2 Listen again and complete Jason's form below. SCAN

Physical Evaluation

Student's Name *Jason Brooks*   Sex *male*   Age *15*

Height ....   Weight ....   Blood pressure ....

Clearance

☐ Apt to practice sports.

☐ Apt after completing rehabilitation for: ....
....

☐ Not apt for: ....

Reason: ....

Recommendation: ....
....

Date: 12/01/2012

Signature: *Gillian M. Rockwell*

As a minimum requirement, this **Physical Examination Form** must be completed prior to junior high athletic participation and again prior to first and third years of high school athletic participation.

3 Answer T (true) or F (false).

a ◯ Jason plays basketball.
b ◯ The doctor thinks Jason is athletic.
c ◯ The doctor thinks basketball is the right sport for Jason's body type.
d ◯ Jason is taking medicine for his allergy.
e ◯ Jason's parents are hypertensive.
f ◯ Jason is apt to play basketball.

4 Is this conversation formal or informal? GENRE

Unit 1 – In all shapes and colors

19

 **Medical evaluation form**

A medical evaluation form is a document that proves that you are healthy to practice sports or to participate in physical activities. You can write the information in the first part of the form. The second part of the form is reserved for the doctor.

Last name: _____

First name: _____

Age: _____   Height: _____   Weight: _____

Are you taking any medications regularly? Yes _____   No _____

If yes, what medications are you taking? _____

_____

Do you wear glasses or contact lenses? Yes _____   No _____

Are you allergic to any medication or food? Yes _____   No _____

If yes, name medication: _____

Do you have any of the following?

a. arthritis Yes _____   No _____

b. diabetes Yes _____   No _____

c. hypertension/high blood pressure Yes _____   No _____

d. high cholesterol Yes _____   No _____

e. asthma Yes _____   No _____

Date: ____/____/____

Signature: _____

Preparing to write

1. Make sure you know your measurements (height, weight) and names of medicines you are taking.

2. Check if you understand the words in the form. If you don't, look them up in a dictionary.

Draft

3. Write the information on the correct lines.
4. Proofread your text.

Final version

5. Check if the information is on the correct lines.
6. Check if your handwriting is clear. The doctor needs to read and understand all the information correctly.

Proofreading

For good handwriting try to:

• write the letters in parallel:
  letters

• write the group of small letters and the group of long letters in the same height:
  acei   bdfh   gj

• keep an equal distance between the letters.

20

Grammar — To be vs. other verbs

1 Complete the sentences with the correct form of the verbs from the box.

> be • like • live • have

a Son: Dad, ... I tall for my age?
Dad: Yes, you .... 7 years old and 1.62 meters tall!
Son: .... you .... to be tall, dad?
Dad: I .... it when I play basketball. I .... it when I buy clothes. It .... easy to find clothes in my size.

b Aaliyah and Katie .... best friends. Aaliyah has black eyes and black hair. Katie .... blue eyes and blond hair. Aaliyah .... long curly hair. Katie .... short straight hair. They .... the same height, but they .... the same weight.

c Guillermo .... from Mexico and he .... in Guadalajara. Guillermo .... a professional wrestler of lucha libre, a very popular sport in Mexico and other Spanish countries. He .... the body of a typical *luchador*: he .... fat and average height. He .... short dark hair and dark eyes.

d My name .... Charlotte and I .... from New Zealand. I .... a lawyer and in my free time I .... a para rugby player. Most rugby players .... athletic and average height. I .... straight red hair and I .... light-skinned.

2 Match the columns according to activity 1.

a In affirmative sentences with the verb *to be* we use…
b In negative sentences with the verb *to be* we use…
c In interrogative sentences with the verb *to be* we use…
d In affirmative sentences with other verbs…
e In negative sentences with other verbs we use…
f In interrogative sentences with other verbs we use…

◯ the verb form changes for *he*, *she*, and *it*.
◯ not after *am*, *is*, and *are*.
◯ not after *do* and *does*.
◯ *am*, *is*, and *are* after the subject.
◯ *do* and *does* before the subject.
◯ the verb before the subject.

Unit 1 – In all shapes and colors

21

3 Complete the conversation appropriately.

Alyson: .... you a cowgirl?

Patsy: Yes, I ....

Alyson: That's so cool! How old .... you?

Patsy: I .... 17.

Alyson: .... you .... in rodeos? (**to compete**)

Patsy: Yes, I .... I .... good at barrel racing.

Alyson: What .... barrel racing?

Patsy: It .... a type of rodeo event.
.... you .... horses? (**to like**)

Alyson: I .... horses, but I .... how to
ride them. (**to like; to know/negative**)

Patsy: .... you .... to meet my horse, Mungo? (**to want**)

Alyson: Sure!

Patsy: He .... aggressive, so you .... to be scared.
(**to be – negative; to have – negative**)

Alyson: Ok. .... he .... sugar? (**to like**)

Patsy: Oh, yeah. He .... sugar, but I .... it to him. I ....
to give him apples. (**to love; to give – negative; to prefer**)

Alyson: I .... an apple with me. Can I .... it to Mungo?
(**to have; to give**)

Patsy: Sure!

> **Remember!**
>
> We usually use contracted forms in dialogues. Example: I'm a tall boy.

4 Make guesses about a classmate and complete the chart.

Student's name _____ **Age** _____
Favorite color _____
Brothers or sisters? ☐ No. ☐ Yes. ____ brother(s) / ____ sister(s).
Favorite food _____
Likes volleyball? ☐ Yes. ☐ No.
Her / His mother works? ☐ Yes. ☐ No.

5 Ask questions to your classmate and confirm your notes.

Are you 12?
Is blue your favorite color?
Do you have any brothers or sisters?

....

....

....

Pronunciation — Stop sounds

The stop sounds are /p/, /b/, /k/, /g/, /t/, and /d/.
They are formed by the air being blocked in the mouth and then released: **pop**, **book**, **coat**, **cup**, **blog**, **end** (and not "popy", "booky", "coaty", "cupy", "blogy", "endy")

1 Listen and repeat. 🎧 5

sport **put** **sprint** **short** **height** **fat** **athletic**
straight **long** **black** **blond** **red** **skinned**

Speaking — Show and tell

1 Bring to the class a photo of someone you admire, **GENRE** like a celebrity or a family member, for example. The photo can be real, from a magazine, newspaper, or a digital one. Talk about the person in your photo to the class. When preparing a show and tell, remember:

- Make notes. They are your guidelines: don't read them, just use them as a reference.
- Start and finish your presentation with interesting, funny, or surprising information to engage your audience's attention.
- Practice before you do it, for example, present it in front of a mirror.

> A **Show and tell** is a common classroom activity very popular in the United States and Australia. It consists of showing something to the class and talking about it. It helps students to develop skills for speaking in public.

Follow these steps for a good Show and tell presentation.
- **Opening:** Greet your audience.
- **Introduction:** Tell your audience the topic of your presentation.
- **Presentation:** Talk about the photo.
- **Closing:** Thank your audience for their attention. Ask if they have any questions.

↑ Road to success

At your own pace

Uma pessoa não é igual a outra, nem todo mundo aprende no mesmo ritmo. Portanto, não se compare a outros alunos.

Cada pessoa tem um ritmo de aprendizagem. Não fique triste porque alguém na sua turma memorizou mais palavras do que você ou cometeu menos erros em uma prova. Seu foco deve ser o que você pode fazer para ser um aluno melhor do que foi na semana anterior.

Peça ajuda ao seu professor e elabore um plano de estudos realista. Seja disciplinado e, pouco a pouco, você notará seu desenvolvimento no idioma e se sentirá mais seguro e confiante para continuar seus estudos.

Unit 1 – In all shapes and colors

Go to *Looking Back* **on page 72** ▶ 23

ITINERARY

In this unit, you will develop the following competences:
- reading an infograph to get general and specific information about puberty;
- learning words and expressions to talk about puberty issues;
- using *should* or *shouldn't* to give advice;
- listening to a news report to get general and specific information about puberty;
- learning the comparative form of adjectives to make comparisons;
- reading about how juggling can improve your coordination;
- listening to different accents to identify British and American varieties;
- reflecting on the effects of puberty in order to deal with it;
- writing a message on an internet forum to get help.

Reading Infographic

Puberty

Puberty is the name for the time when your body begins to develop and change as you move from being a kid to being an adult. Usually, puberty starts between ages 8 and 13 in girls and ages 10 and 15 in boys.

(1) When your body is ready to begin puberty, your **pituitary gland** releases special hormones. These hormones go to work on different parts of the boy's and girl's bodies.

(2) These hormones change the way your body looks on the outside and they also create changes on the inside.

Central Nervous System

(3) During puberty, you can have mood swings and problems with coordination of movements. It's important to know that while your body is adjusting to the new hormones, your mind is adjusting to them too. It's only natural, so be patient and don't panic!

Pimples show up everywhere on his and her face.

Voice gets lower.

The body becomes more muscular.

Breasts develop.

The body develops curves.

Hips grow wider.

- Hair grows under their arms and on their pubic areas (on and around the genitals). Hair also starts to grow on his face.

- For boys, the hormones tell the **testes** to begin making testosterone and sperm. Testosterone is the hormone that causes most of the changes in a boy's body during puberty, and men need sperm to be able to reproduce (to be the father of a baby).

- In girls, these hormones affect the **ovaries**. The hormones cause the ovaries to start making another hormone, called estrogen. Together, these hormones prepare a girl's body to start her periods and be able to become pregnant someday.

26

1 Infographics (information graphics) are visual representations of information, data, or knowledge. Complete the sentences about infographics with the words below. {GENRE}

story • fun • difficult • colors • websites • images

a Infographics are everywhere: in magazines, newspapers, on posters, ..., etc.

b Infographics simplify things that sometimes are too .... to explain with a text.

c A lot of people prefer to read infographics because they are .... and easy to understand.

d Infographics have more .... than text. Texts are simple and objective.

e Infographics often use different .... and fonts to be more attractive.

f Very frequently, infographics tell a .... with pictures.

2 What is the subject of this infographic? {SKIM}

○ Sexual education.   ○ The reproductive system.   ○ Puberty.

3 Read the infographic and answer. {SCAN}

a What is puberty?

○ It is when we become adults.

○ It is the period when our bodies change.

○ It is the period when our bodies begin to develop.

b The hormone that causes most of the changes in a woman's body is called…

○ estrogen.   ○ testosterone.

c The hormone that causes most of the changes in a man's body is called…

○ estrogen.   ○ testosterone.

4 Write B for boys, G for girls, and BG for boys and girls.

○ voice changes   ○ emotions are affected by hormones

○ hips become wider   ○ pimples become more common

○ breasts develop   ○ curves appear

○ muscles develop   ○ hair grows under arms and on pubic areas

YOUR TAKE

1. Do you have mood swings?

....

2. What about problems with coordination of movements?

....

Unit 2 – I'm going through changes

Vocabulary  Puberty issues

1 Check these words related to puberty then listen and repeat them.

use pads

gain weight

outgrow your clothes

shave

feel embarassed

wear a bra

get pimples

use deodorant

2 Complete the table below with the vocabulary above.

If you are a girl...	If you are a boy...	Both of you:
a. you get your period and start to	d. hair starts to grow on your face and you start to	g. hair grows under your arm and you start to ....
b. your breasts develop and you start to	e. your voice cracks and you	h. you............................ on your face because of hormonal changes
c. your body develops curves and you	f. your body becomes more muscular and you	

28

Speaking  Giving advice

1 Listen and read.

A: I have pimples all over my face. What should I do?

B: You should <u>wash your face very well twice a day</u>.

B: You shouldn't <u>pop your pimples, they can get infected</u>.

A: OK, thanks for the advice.

2 Work with a partner. Follow the instructions below.

  a **Student A:** You are having some problems. Talk to Student B and ask for advice.
  Student B: Go to page 148.

PROBLEMS
- I feel embarrassed in PE classes because I'm very uncoordinated.
- All the girls in my class are wearing bras, but I'm not.
- I have mood swings and I can't control my emotions.
- I have doubts about sex.

  b **Student A:** Student B is having some problems. Listen to them and choose the best advice to give him / her.

ADVICE

YES
- Use deodorant every day.
- Wait and be patient. Voice changes are usually fast.
- See a gynecologist to learn more about your periods.
- Eat healthy food and exercise.

NO
- Shave without the help of an adult.
- Feel embarrassed. This situation is temporary and normal.
- Use the same pad for more than 4 hours.
- Go on a diet without the help of a doctor or nutritionist.

3 Tell your partner about a real problem you have at the moment and ask for advice. Remember to thank him / her.

Unit 2 – I'm going through changes

Listening — In the news

1 Listen to this news report about a study on puberty and complete the sentences. 🎧12 SKIM

   a A new study shows that more ……………………………… girls are starting puberty at a younger age.

   b Scientists found early breast development in ……………………………… -year-old girls.

   c ……………………………… and ……………………………… substances are the probable causes.

2 Listen again and answer. 🎧12 SCAN

   a What is estrogen?

     ◯ It is the hormone responsible for the female reproductive system.

     ◯ It is the hormone responsible for obesity in girls.

   b Substances in plastic and fertilizers can simulate estrogen in our bodies.

     ◯ true   ◯ false

   c What should we do to prevent this problem?

     ◯ Have a balanced diet.

     ◯ Eat industrialized food.

     ◯ Have an active life.

Grammar — Comparative form

1 Read the sentence below and do the activities.

During puberty the body becomes more muscular and we get taller.

a What's the sentence comparing?

....

b Complete:

In the first part of the sentence, we use .... + adjective and in the second part we use adjective + ...

c What's your conclusion? Complete with **short** or **long**.

To make comparatives, we use **more** when the adjective is a .... word and we use **-er** when the adjective is a .... word.

2 Write the adjectives below in the correct column.

low * wide * difficult
big * heavy * funny
beautiful * interesting
easy * small * boring
athletic * slim * cute

Short adjectives	Long adjectives
....	....
....	....
....	....

3 Read the examples and complete the spelling rules for short adjectives.

a I'm **slimmer** than my sister.

b In my opinion, English is **easier** than Portuguese.

c The girls' hips grow **wider** during puberty.

For adjectives ending in **consonant, vowel, consonant**, we double the last .... + **-er** to form the comparative. Another adjective that follows this rule is ....

For adjectives ending in **-y**, we remove the **-y** and include .... to form the comparative. Another adjective that follows this rule is ....

For adjectives ending in **-e**, we only include .... to form the comparative. Another adjective that follows this rule is ....

Unit 2 – I'm going through changes

31

4 Complete the testimonies with the comparatives.

My name is Marcus and I'm 13 years old. My body is getting .... (big) and .... (heavy) so it's .... (easy) for me to gain weight now. During PE classes, there are some exercises that are .... (difficult) for me because I'm feeling a little uncoordinated.

My name is Zoe and I'm 12 years old. My hips are starting to grow .... (wide) and I'm growing .... (tall), so I'm outgrowing my clothes very fast. My body isn't .... (muscular), but I think I'm .... (slim) now.

5 Are you in puberty? Give your testimonial.

....
....
....
....
....

Physical Education  English

1 **In your PE classes, do you do exercises to practice coordination? Which exercises?**

Coordination is the harmonious use of your body in the execution of movements. During puberty teenagers usually have problems with their coordination. PE classes (Physical Education) offer them the possibility to use their bodies in balance.
Some sports can help you develop your eye-hand coordination (such as tennis and baseball), but there are other activities that you can practice at home, like juggling, for example.

2 **Learn and practice the three-ball juggling.**

Can you maintain three balls in the air, tossing and catching them repeatedly? It takes practice, repetition, and patience, but you can do it!

1 Start with one ball (or an orange). Toss it up from your left hand to your right hand and vice-versa. Try to maintain the ball at the level of your eyes.

3 Use three balls. Hold one ball in your right hand and two in the left hand. Throw one of the two balls in your left hand to your right hand. At the same time, throw the ball in your right hand to your left hand and repeat the process. Keep one ball always moving in the air.

2 Use two balls. Holding one ball in each hand, throw the ball from your right hand to your left hand, but before you catch the ball in your left hand, throw the other ball to your right hand. Do the same starting with your left hand. Remember: the balls have to be at the level of your eyes. Only go to **step 3** after you dominate **step 2**.

4 You are juggling! With more practice, you can try with 4 balls. Or move to rings and pins!

REFLECT
1. In your opinion, why is coordination practice important during puberty?

33

Pronunciation — You say tomato, I say "tomahto"

There are many differences between American and British pronunciation.
One of these differences is the "absent R".

1 Listen to an American person reading these words. 🎧 8
   wider / lower / taller / bigger

2 Now listen to a British person reading the same words. 🎧 9
   wider / lower / taller / bigger

The British speaker doesn't enunciate the letter *r*, but makes a long *ah* sound.
This also happens with words ending in **-ar**, **-or**, **-ere**, **-air**, and **-ear**.

3 Listen and repeat these words to practice both pronunciations. 🎧 10

smaller   cheaper   car
favor   there   fair   dear

4 Listen and answer: American or British? 🎧 11

a taller   ○ American   ○ British
b car   ○ American   ○ British
c dear   ○ American   ○ British
d favor   ○ American   ○ British
e smaller   ○ American   ○ British

↑ Road to success

Dealing with puberty

A puberdade é uma fase de muitas mudanças físicas e alterações emocionais. Pode afetar sua concentração nas aulas não apenas por causa das mudanças no seu ritmo biológico, mas também pela descoberta de novos interesses. Como se isso já não fosse o bastante, pesquisas recentes indicam que as mudanças na estrutura do cérebro que ocorrem durante a puberdade diminuem a capacidade de aprendizagem.
Mas não use a puberdade como desculpa para o seu mau desempenho na escola. As ferramentas mais importantes para o aprendizado são a sua determinação e a sua persistência. Se estiver com algum problema, converse com seus pais, seus professores ou um orientador pedagógico. Eles já passaram por essa fase e podem lhe dar conselhos muito úteis.

Writing

A message in an internet forum

An internet forum is an online site where people talk by posting messages about an specific topic.

Complete the question of an imaginary forum about puberty.

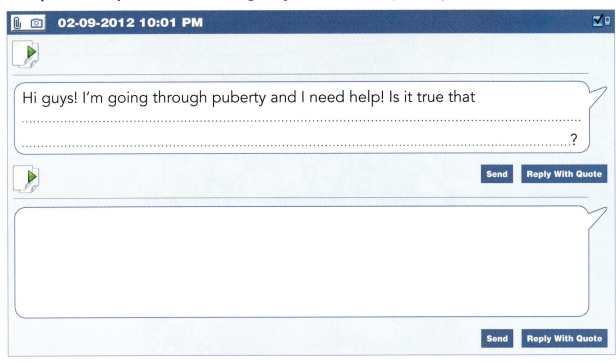

Now give your book to a classmate.

Preparing to write
1. What does the person who wrote the message want to know?
2. Do you have the answer to his / her question? Do some research before you answer.

Draft
3. Write your reply on a separate piece of paper. Give answers, suggestions, or advice.
4. Proofread your text.

Final version
5. Write your reply in your classmate's book.

Share
6. Before you return your classmate's book, show your reply to another classmate and ask for his / her opinion: Is the reply clear? Can he / she suggest any improvement in your reply?
7. Return your classmate's book.

Proofreading TIP

When you write an argumentative text, you need to follow this organization model: introduction, body, conclusion. You usually need one paragraph for the introduction, one, two, or three for the body, and one for the conclusion.

166

Go to *Looking Back* on page 72 ▶ 35

Stopover Units 1 & 2

1 Guess who. Read these descriptions and name the people in the family.

Louise doesn't have black, brown, blond, or red hair.
Daniel is short. He is younger than **Andre** and **Sarah**.
Patrick and **Alfred** are chubby.
Alfred is older than **Patrick**. He doesn't have blond hair.
Andre has long arms. He doesn't have brown hair.
Eric isn't short. He is taller than **Patrick**. His hair is not black, brown or blond.
Anne has long curly hair. She is married to **Alfred**.
Nadia and **Sarah** have the same hair style. But **Nadia** is older than **Sarah**.
Ned is a little taller than **Jacob**, but **Jacob** is heavier than **Ned**.
Jacob doesn't have blond hair.
Paul is older than **Louise**.
Alfred and **Paul** have short hair.

2 Order this conversation.

○ Jen: Put the vinegar and sodium bicarbonate in the container and wait… Wow!
○ Pedro: OK, goggles on. Now read the instructions, Jen.
○ Pedro: Do you know what happens?
○ Jen: We have to test what happens when we mix these two ingredients.
○ Jen: No, I don't. Let's start and see.
○ Malcolm: Wait! Is it safe? Do we have to wear protection?
○ Jen: Vinegar and sodium bicarbonate.
○ Malcolm: Really cool! But… now we have to clean the table…
○ Jen: Yes, good idea. Let's wear these goggles.
1 Pedro: Ok, Jen. What do we have to do?
○ Pedro: Oh, my God! It's like an eruption of a volcano! That's cool!
○ Malcolm: What are the ingredients?

3 Interview a classmate and complete the table.

Questions	Classmate's answers
What is your ……………………………………….?	
What are your favorite …………………………….?	
What do you like to eat …………………………….?	
What do you do after …………………………….?	
Who is your favorite …………………………….?	
Do you ……………………………………. in the morning?	
Is ……………………………. your favorite color?	
Are your parents …………………………………….?	
…………………………….? (write your own question)	

Stopover   37

Extra Reading 1

1 **What do you know about acne? Answer T (true) or F (false).**

a ◯ Acne is a signal of puberty.

b ◯ You have to be 10, 11, 12, or 13 years old to have acne.

c ◯ Girls usually have acne first.

d ◯ Acne problems in girls are usually more serious than in boys.

e ◯ Acne disappears after you are 20 years old.

f ◯ There is nothing you can do to treat acne.

2 **Read the excerpt from the book _Acne For Dummies_, By Herbert P. Goodheart, M.D. and check your answers in activity 1.**

Chapter **4**

Examining Acne in Teens

In teenagers, acne is one of the signals that your body is going through a tremendous upheaval called puberty. Teenage acne often begins around the ages of 10 to 13. It may start before puberty in both sexes, but teenage girls tend to start getting acne at a younger age than boys; however, boys tend to have the more severe cases. Studies have shown that puberty is occurring at an earlier age these days, and so is acne. Most teenagers grow out of it when they reach 19 or 20; however, don't be surprised if your acne persists into your early 20s and even into later adulthood.

But just because acne is common and almost every teen suffers through it doesn't mean you can't do anything about it. You don't have to just wait for it to go away. That's what I'm here for — to help you knock out those pimples, whiteheads, and blackheads. With so many excellent acne treatments available today, treating your acne will prevent (or at least greatly lessen) the scarring that often results from untreated acne.

GOODHEART, H. P. *Acne For Dummies*. Hobokes,
NJ: John Wileys & Sons, 2004.

3 Read again and answer.

   a Why do you have to treat acne?
   ....
   ....

   b Why are studies about puberty showing these days?
   ....
   ....

   c Is acne a problem for teenagers only?
   ....
   ....
   ....

4 Match.

A. scar   B. lessen   C. pimples

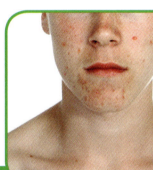

5 Find in the text words that mean:

   a a violent change ....
   b the period in life after adolescence ....
   c to eliminate ....

6 The author mentions **whiteheads** and **blackheads**. Look at the explanation below. What do you think they are? INFER

Formation of Skin Whiteheads and Blackheads

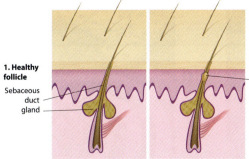
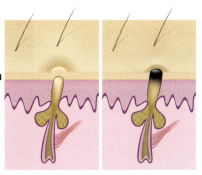

1. Healthy follicle
   Sebaceous duct gland

2. Duct clogged by dead cells, sebum starts to accumulate

3. Whitehead formed underneath skin surface

4. Blackhead formed when sebum plug is opened to skin surface and oxidized

Extra Reading 1   39

Project 1

The Dexterity Game

> Besides video games, what other games do you like to play?

1 Games are divided into many categories. How many games can you name in each of these categories?

street games | paper and pencil games | guessing games | board games | card games

Board games	Paper and pencil games	Card games	Street games	Guessing games
....	....	....	....	....
....	....	....	....	....
....	....	....	....	....
....	....	....	....	....

2 A very popular category of games is called dexterity games, which involve manual dexterity or hand-eye coordination. Which of these pictures show dexterity games?

a b

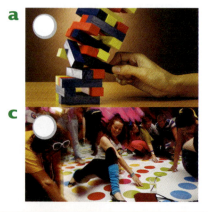
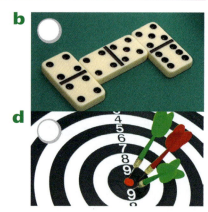

c d

40 Units 1 & 2

3 **You and your group are going to build a dexterity game together (like the item c in activity 2).**

  a Gather the material you'll need:
  - A piece of fabric or canvas of a light color (an old bed sheet, for example) measuring 1.7m x 1.40m
  - Paint (4 different colors) and brushes
  - Glue and scissors
  - A pen

  b Then, make the mat. Using the brushes and the paint, paint your fabric like this (use the colors you chose):

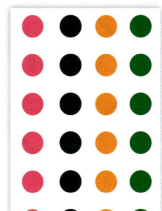

  c Copy the cube model below twice, on two separate sheets of paper:
  - On one copy, write the name of a different part of the body in each square.
  - On the other copy, write the names of the 4 colors on your mat.
  - On the other two squares, write "Your choice".
  - Cut out the models and glue them to form two dice.

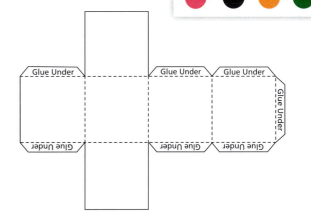

  d If necessary, your game can also be adapted to classmates with special needs:
  - Draw shapes (oval, rectangle, triangle, and star) instead of using colors. Some people can't see colors.
  - Cut out circles from different fabrics with textures (fur, leather, carpet, etc.) and glue each circle in the mat. Blind people can play this game using their touch, instead of their sight.
  - Hang your mat on the wall instead of putting it on the floor and use only parts of the upper body on the dice. Handicapped people can play this game using their arms and head. In this case, you can make the mat with more spaced circles and test flexibility instead of balance.

4 **Let's play!** Your teacher will help you with the rules of the game. While you are playing, use these sentences to communicate:

> Your turn! / My turn!
> Can you repeat that, please?
> I give up!
> I win!

5 After you play the game, answer: how do you evaluate your dexterity and coordination skills, considering your performance in this game? Why?

....
....
....
....

Project 1

UNIT 3
Technology

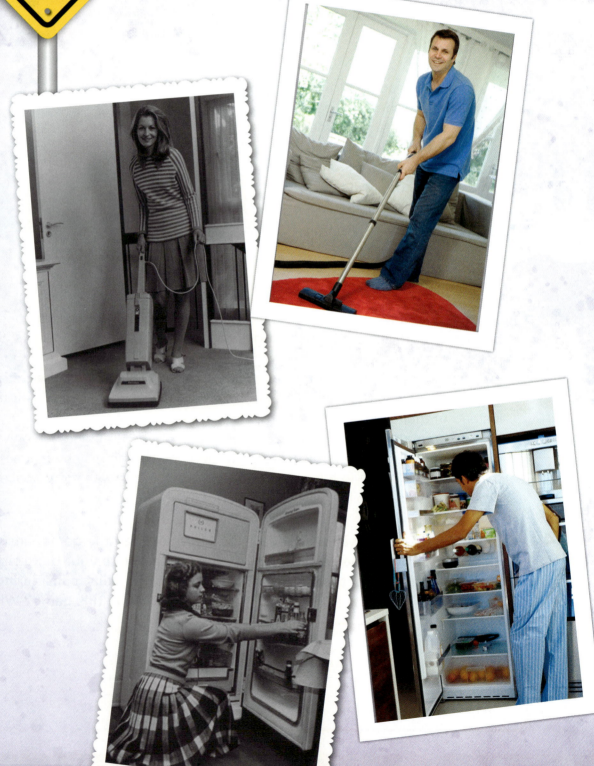

ITINERARY

In this unit, you will develop the following competences:
- reading an advertisement to get general and specific information about an old electronic device;
- learning words and expressions to talk about technology problems;
- using *used to* and its correct pronunciation to talk about habits in the past;
- expressing doubt and disbelief to talk about old gadgets;
- reading about bits and bytes to understand how the binary system works;
- thinking about how to use technology to learn English;
- listening to a customer calling a call center to get general and specific information about product assistance;
- completing an online form to get support for a product.

Reading — An electronics advertisement

1 Write the names for each category below.

: equipment & parts   power supply   weight :

AC power cord   batteries   car battery cord

featherweight

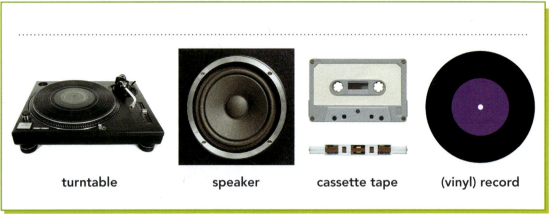

turntable   speaker   cassette tape   (vinyl) record

2 Press ads appear in newspapers, magazines, or specific publications. **GENRE**
Choose the best options to complete the sentences.

a The main objective of a press ad is to…
- ◯ generate consumption of a product or service.
- ◯ educate and motivate the public about important issues.

b The basic elements of a good press ad are…
- a title that calls the attention of the…   ◯ reader.   ◯ company.
- a picture (or illustration) that relates to the…   ◯ headline.   ◯ date of publication.
- a text that explains the benefits of the…   ◯ magazine.   ◯ product.
- the brand of the company that makes…   ◯ the magazine.   ◯ the product.

c A good commercial press ad uses…
- ◯ formal and correct language.
- ◯ language that the readers understand and connect to.

3 Read the advertising and answer the questions.

Glossary

hold: support with your hand
built-in: integral part of the equipment
perhaps: maybe
yet: up to the present time

Sorry, no turntable.

You're looking at the Sony Soundabout AM/FM Stereo Cassette-Corder.
As the name implies, it offers AM/FM stereo, it records and plays back cassettes.
This little machine does everything your home stereo does. Except play records.
It took major technological advances in micro-circuitry to pack so much into an audio system that you could hold in one hand.
So why talk about what this Stereo Cassette-Corder doesn't have? Perhaps it's because we've always believed the impossible is possible.
No, it doesn't have a turntable.
Yet.

© 1982 Sony Corporation of America. Sony, Soundabout and Cassette-Corder are trademarks of Sony Corporation. Model shown: WA-55   **SONY** THE ONE AND ONLY

a What does the equipment offer?
- ◯ AM / FM stereo.
- ◯ Cassette recording.
- ◯ Cassette playing.
- ◯ Record playing.

b What is included in the equipment?
- ◯ Power supply.
- ◯ Speaker.
- ◯ Antenna.
- ◯ Turntable.
- ◯ Microphone.
- ◯ Headphones.

4 Answer T (true) or F (false).
- ◯ This machine does everything that a home stereo does.
- ◯ Technological advances made the small model possible.
- ◯ The "corder" part of the name refers to the fact that it records and plays cassette tapes.

5 Why does the advertisement start with the sentence "Sorry, no turntable" and end with "No, it doesn't have a turntable. Yet."?   **INFER**

....

....

Unit 3 – Technology

45

Vocabulary Technology problems

1 Read and listen to the sentences. Then match the sentences with the pictures. 🎧13

1 My old phone always **loses the signal**.
2 This software doesn't **run** on this operating system.
3 My batteries **are dead**.
4 My phone **doesn't get a good reception** in the school.
5 I have a 1Mb **broadband connection**.
6 There is no free space in my **flash drive**.
7 The left earphone **is not working**.
8 Is there a **wireless connection** in the rooms?
9 My computer frequently **crashes**.

2 Complete the sentences with the vocabulary from activity one.

a  I can't hear anything. I don't think my earphones are ....

b Mirian: I want to make a call, but my cell phone battery is ....
Ana: Do you want to use my cell phone?
Mirian: Thanks, but we don't get .... in subway stations.
Cecilia: Really? My cell phone never .... when I am on the train.

c  Vitor: I want to install the same software you use to edit photos.
Carol: But you can't use this software because your computer .... another operating system.

d Ivan: We can use the .... in the shopping mall.
Fernando: But I can't connect without a password.

e  Heloise: Save the document, please.
Renata: Oh, yes. I hate it when the computer .... and we lose all the work!
Heloise: Just to be safe, save it in my .... , too. There is a lot of free space.

f Rose: Can we upload files at the same time?
Lucas: Sure. I have a .... It isn't a problem.

Unit 3 – Technology

47

Grammar *Used to*

🔊 166

1 Read the sentences below.

In the 70s, remote controls used to be big and have few buttons.

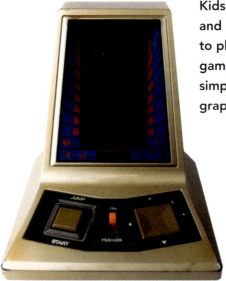

Kids in the 70s and 80s used to play video games with very simple and poor graphics.

Before CDs and flash drives, people used to store information on floppy disks.

2 Answer.

   a Are the sentences about the present, past, or future?

   ....

   b The expression **used to** talks about…
   - ◯ habit or routine in the past.
   - ◯ something that only happened once.

   c The sentences with **used to** follow the order…
   - ◯ *used to* + main verb + object + subject.
   - ◯ subject + *used to* + main verb.
   - ◯ subject + *used to* + object.

3 Complete the sentences with **used to** and the correct verb from the box.

> show • make • have • buy • pay • be

   a The first video cassette players .... big and slow.

   b Cassette tapes .... colorful packages.

c In the past, people .... photos with a slide projector.

d Before telephone cards, people .... for public phone calls with tokens.

e In the past, people .... heavy and uncomfortable mouses.

f Your grandparents .... copies using a mimeograph.

Pronunciation *Used to*

1 **Listen and answer.**
   I **used to** live in an apartment.
   ◯ use**d t**o = sound of *z*   ◯ use**d t**o = sound of *t*
   ◯ use**d t**o = sound of *s*   ◯ use**d t**o = sound of *d*

2 **Listen and repeat.**
   a She used to have long hair.
   b They used to walk to school.
   c I used to help my father at work.
   d You used to be sleepy all the time.

Unit 3 – Technology

49

Speaking — Expressing doubt and showing disbelief

1 Two friends are talking about an old object they found. Listen to the conversation. 🎧16

A: What is it?
B: <u>I have no idea.</u>
A: This is an old car radio.
B: <u>No way! I can't believe it!</u>

Expressing doubt	
I have no idea.	I don't have a clue.

Showing disbelief	
Really?	Are you for real?
No kidding!	I can't believe it!
Are you serious?	Come on!
No way!	Get out of here!

2 Can you identify these old gadgets? Talk to your partner and comment about them.

a. Video camera, b. Radio, c. Tape recorder, d. Telephone, e. Record player, f. Freezer.

3 Talk about your past. Mention something surprising about you. Talk about things you used to like, places you used to go to, TV shows you used to watch, etc.

Bits & bytes

We usually use the decimal code in our day-to-day activities. The decimal code uses ten digits (0,1,2,3,4,5,6,7,8,9), but there are other ways to represent numbers.

Computers, for example, use a different system. They use electrical impulses to process information. If the impulse is off, it represents 0. If it is on, it represents 1. A digit that can be either 0 or 1 is called a bit (represented by b). And this is a binary code.

```
11010011010011010111001010001101100
0010110010110001011100010101110010
10101000100011101000110101101010100
```

Compare:

Decimal Number	Binary Number
0	0
1	1
2	10
3	11
4	100
5	101
6	110
7	111
8	1000
9	1001
10	1010
11	1011

Because bits are very small, they are usually grouped into eight bits to form a **byte** (represented by B).

$$8 \text{ b} = 1 \text{ B}$$

When operating with multiples of bytes, computers use this system:

$$1{,}024 \text{ B} = 1 \text{ KB}$$
$$1{,}024 \text{ KB} = 1 \text{ MB}$$
$$1{,}024 \text{ MB} = 1 \text{ GB}$$

Why is it important to know that?

When you buy a 1 GB flash drive and insert it in your computer it shows only 0.93 GB!

This is because the hardware companies use a **decimal number system** to define storage space, but the computer uses a **binary system**.

Hardware Companies: 1,000 B = 1 MB
Computers: 1,024 B = 1 MB

YOUR TAKE

1. Do you think hardware companies have to inform the customers about this difference? Why?
....
....

2. If you have 1 GB of files to save on a flash drive, how big should it be?
( ) 1MB.   ( ) 1GB.   ( ) 2GB.

In the movie *The Matrix*, the streaming lines of green computer code are binary numbers.

↑ Road to success

Using technology to learn English

Aprender um idioma é uma tarefa que exige dedicação e estudo, independentemente dos materiais que você usar. A tecnologia pode ajudá-lo a fazer isso de modo mais fácil e agradável.

Algumas simples mudanças podem fazer uma grande diferença. Você pode, por exemplo, alterar o idioma dos seus aparelhos eletrônicos para o inglês. Assim, sempre que utilizar celulares, MP3 *players*, aparelhos de GPS, televisores etc., estará interagindo com eles em inglês.

Você também pode usar recursos como o SAP (*second audio program*), disponível em alguns aparelhos de TV, e opções de legendas em inglês, que você vai encontrar na maioria dos DVDs.

E no computador, que tal instalar programas em inglês?

Listening — Calling a call center

When you have a problem with some equipment that you buy, you can contact a call center. A call center is an office created to receive a big number of telephone calls, especially for taking orders and giving customer service.

1 Answer. `GENRE`

   a When you call a call center, you talk to…
   - ◯ a machine.
   - ◯ a person.
   - ◯ a machine or a person.

   b Clients call the call center to…
   - ◯ ask questions about a product or service.
   - ◯ sell a product.
   - ◯ complain about a product or service.
   - ◯ ask for assistance.

2 Listen to the conversation and check the correct options. 🎧17 `SKIM`

   a Who is calling the call center?
   - ◯ Alice.   ◯ Anthony.

   b What is the problem?
   - ◯ The battery is dead after some hours of use.
   - ◯ The Bluetooth does not work.
   - ◯ The wi-fi and GPS are not working.

   c Is the problem resolved in the end?
   - ◯ Yes.   ◯ No.

3 Listen again and answer. 🎧17 `SCAN`

   a How does the representative know that the cell phone has the Bluetooth, wi-fi, and GPS features?

   ....

   b Does the customer know his cell phone well?

   ....

52

 **Online customer support form**

Preparing to write

1. You're having problems with an electronic device, and you need to contact the company that produced the device via the Internet. What's the name of the company?
2. What's wrong with the product?
3. You reach the online customer support in the company's website. Look at the form below. What information about the product do you need to know?

Draft

4. On a separate sheet of paper, describe to the company the problem you're having with your device. Give details.
5. Ask the company for a solution or for help.
6. Proofread your text.

Final version

7. Complete the form and include the description of the problem.

| Support home | Find your product | Softwares and drivers | Service information | Online Store | Contact |

Contact us
Have your questions answered by email.

Model category: ☐ cell phone   ☐ TV   ☐ DVD player   ☐ MP3 player
                 ☐ laptop computer   ☐ other: _____

Model number: _____
Date of purchase: _____
Description of the problem: _____

Last name: _____
First name: _____
Email address: _____

Share

8. Imagine that before you contact the company's technical support, you decide to post your problem on an internet forum. Read your classmates' problems and write back if you have a solution for his / her problem.

Proofreading TIP

When you describe a problem, it is useful to organize your explanation with sequencing words. Start your description with *first* or *first of all*. Continue your story with *next*, *then*, or *after that*. Finish it with expressions like *lastly* or *finally*.

Go to *Looking Back* on page 73

Almanac mania

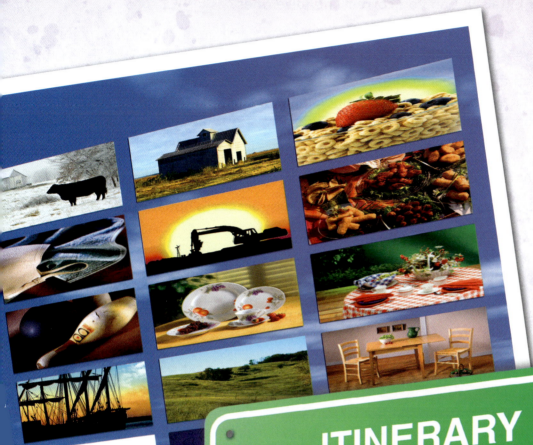

ITINERARY

In this unit, you will develop the following competences:
- reading an almanac page to get general and specific information about the 1990s;
- learning words to talk about almanac sections;
- using the verb *to be* in the past to talk about previous decades;
- practicing the reduction of the verb *to be* and subject pronouns to ask questions in the past;
- listening to a TV game show to get general and specific information about it;
- reading about the presidents of Brazil to learn more about them and then doing some research;
- reflecting on the development of your English skills to focus on what you still need to improve;
- using expressions to agree or disagree;
- writing an entry to publish in a class almanac.

Reading: The 90s in an almanac

1 Write T (true) or F (false). Can you correct the false ones? [GENRE]

a ◯ An almanac is a publication that contains statistics and general information for a specific year or decade.

b ◯ Some topics that appear in almanacs are geography, government and international affairs, demographics, agriculture, economics, medicine, religion, mass media, transportation, science, technology, sports, awards, and prizes.

c ◯ The content of an almanac is always presented in lists.

d ◯ Only students read almanacs because they can help with school work.

e ◯ People read almanacs because they provide easy access to updated information.

2 Learn how to read years and decades in English.

1500 – fifteen hundred
1635 – sixteen thirty-five
1982 – nineteen eighty-two
2005 – two thousand five
2011 – two thousand eleven

1941-1950 – the 40s (forties)
1971-1980 – the 70s (seventies)
2001-2010 – the two thousands (US) / the noughties (UK)

3 Read this almanac page and complete the sentence on the next page.

The nineties were the decade of technology with the rise to prominence of the personal computer, cellular phone, MP3, and PalmPilot. Though info-age technologies pre-date the '80s, it wasn't until the late 1980s and the 1990s that they became widely used by the public. But perhaps the single most important advance was the growth of the information superhighway: the Internet. In international relations, the 1990s started with the Gulf War (1990-1991) with thirty-four nations, including the United States as leader, against Iraq in response to Iraq's invasion of Kuwait. The decade ended with the whole world preparing for the millennium bug.

In 1989, 15% of American homes had a computer. And by 2000, this figure increased to 51%, with 41.5% online.

The top 5 films of the decade were *Titanic*, *Star Wars Episode I: The Phantom Menace*, *Jurassic Park*, *Independence Day* and *The Lion King*.

Brazil (1994) and France (1998) were the winners of the Football World Cups of the decade.

"The Rachel hairstyle" (from Jennifer Aniston's character on the hit TV show *Friends*) was a cultural phenomenon with millions of women copying it worldwide.

Dolly (1996-2003) was a female domestic sheep and the first mammal to be cloned. She was born on July 5th 1996, in Scotland, and she lived until the age of six.

Adapted from KCLibrary.Lonestar.edu, en.Wikipedia.org, BlogCDN.com

56

The page of the almanac is about... **SKIM**

- ◯ the millennium.
- ◯ the 1990s.
- ◯ this decade.
- ◯ the 2000s.

4 **Which topics does the text mention?** **SCAN**

- ◯ culture
- ◯ economics
- ◯ transportation
- ◯ geography
- ◯ medicine
- ◯ technology
- ◯ demographics
- ◯ religion
- ◯ science
- ◯ agriculture
- ◯ mass media
- ◯ sports
- ◯ awards & prizes
- ◯ government and international affairs

5 **Match the numbers with what they refer to.**

a 51%   **b** 6   **c** 1998   **d** millions

◯ France was the winner of the World Cup this year.

◯ The number of homes with a computer by the year 2000.

◯ F·R·I·E·N·D·S
The number of women who copied "The Rachel hairstyle".

◯ The age Dolly was in 2003.

6 **According to the text, the most important event of the '90s was...**

- **a** ◯ the Gulf War.
- **b** ◯ the millennium bug.
- **c** ◯ the popularization of the Internet.

Unit 4 – Almanac mania

57

Vocabulary

Almanac topics

1 Match the words with the corresponding pictures. Then listen and check your work. 🎧18

> trends • first aid • military • traffic • unemployment
> birth rate • rivers and lakes • weather

....

....

....

....

....

....

....

....

58

2 Complete the tables with the words from activity 1.

Geography	Government and international affairs	Demographics	Economics
maps	regime	immigration	agriculture
flags	constitution	race & ethnicity	energy

Medicine	Mass media	Transportation	Science
health	TV & movies	bridges & tunnels	
	celebrities		environment
diet & nutrition		roads & railways	astronomy

3 Complete these dialogs with words from **activity 1**.

a A: Where can I find information about the Amazon in this almanac?

B: In the section about ...., probably.

b A: What are the temperature records of Brazil?

B: I have no idea. Do some research about the .... in Brazil.

c A: I think these .... and .... statistics are not correct.

B: You should check them on a census website before you use them in your homework.

d A: What does the dictionary say about ".."?

B: That it's the basic medical treatment when someone has a health problem or accident.

e A: This article says that 3D video games are a new ....

B: New??? There's something wrong! When is this article from?

A: Oh… let's see… you're right, it's from 2010.

f A: According to the almanac, during World War II approximately 11,200,000 people served in the U.S. .... (4,200,000 served in the Navy and 660,000 in the Marines.)

B: Wow, that's a lot of people!

g A: Where can I find information or statistics about cars, pollution, bikes, and ....?

B: There is a section about transportation in this book.

167

Unit 4 – Almanac mania

59

Grammar Verb *to be* – past

1 Read the examples. Then complete the sentences.

I was born in 1995. The 90s were the decade of technology.

In the 18th century, nitric acid was the product used in teeth whitening.

The original meaning of the word hospital was "place of hospitality".

Were cosmetics common in ancient times?
Yes. Cosmetics were used by the Egyptians in 400 B.C.

Hairstyles were very different in the past.

Board games were very popular in the 50s and 60s.

a The past form of **am** is ....
b The past form of **is** is ....
c The past form of **are** is ....
d We use .... with **I**, **he**, **she**, **it**.
e We use .... with **you**, **we**, **they**.
f The negative forms of the verb **to be** in the past are .... and ....

2 Answer the questions.
a Where were you born? ....
b When were you born? ....
c Was your grandmother born in Brazil? ....
d When was your best friend born? ....

3 Stella and her grandfather Boris are looking at old photos. Complete their dialog with the past form of the verb *to be*.

Stella: Who .... these children?
Boris: That is me! It .... in Russia. You know that I .... born there, right?
Stella: Oh, really? And who .... the girl?
Boris: That .... a friend's sister.
Stella: Do you remember her name?
Boris: Yes. It .... Olga.
Stella: And who .... the people on the motorcycle?
Boris: Ah, they .... our neighbors. It .... my motorcycle.
Stella: And .... this your car?
Boris: No, no. That .... the neighbor's car. We .... rich, Stella. Cars and motorcycles used to be very expensive at that time.
Stella: I think life .... very different in Russia.
Boris: Oh, yes. But those days .... good.

Pronunciation — Reduction of *was* + subject pronoun

1 Listen to these phrases. Pay attention to the pronunciation of the underlined words. 🎧19
  a <u>Was he</u> at home at 7 am?
  b <u>Was she</u> quiet when she was a child?
  c Are you talking about the rock concert? <u>Was it</u> good?

2 Listen and repeat. 🎧20
  a Was it cold in the morning?
  b Was she happy with the good news?
  c Was he at school yesterday?

was he = /wəzi/ (sound of z; sound of h not pronounced)
was she = /wəʃi/ (sound of s)
was it = /wəzɪt/ (sound of z)

Unit 4 – Almanac mania

61

Listening   A TV game show

1 Mark the correct alternative(s). [GENRE]

a A game show is a type of…
   ○ radio program.
   ○ newspaper.
   ○ television program.

b Who participates in game shows?
   ○ Members of the audience.
   ○ Famous people.
   ○ Groups of people or teams.
   ○ Professional game show players.

c What do they have to do in game shows?
   ○ Answer questions.
   ○ Solve problems or challenges.
   ○ Participate in competitions.
   ○ Buy products.

d What do they get for participating?
   ○ Money.
   ○ Prizes (trips, products, services, etc.).
   ○ Jobs on TV.

2 Listen to this TV game show and answer. [SKIM]
   The questions of this game show are about…
   ○ one topic.   ○ many topics.

3 Listen again and answer. 🎧21   [SCAN]

   a How many contestants are there? ....
   b What are their professions? ....
   c Are they all American? ....
   d How much is the total prize? ....
   e Which was the first country to have paper money? ....
   f Which was the first country to have a woman president? ....
   g Which was the first country to have animal protection laws in
      its Constitution? ....

Crossroads

History of Brazil / English

1 How many Brazilian presidents do you remember without looking at the list below?

The Proclamation of the Republic is celebrated on November 15th to remember the day in 1889 when Emperor Dom Pedro II was deposed and the United States of Brazil was declared by Field Marshal Deodoro da Fonseca, who was the first president of Brazil. Since then, there have been 37 presidents of Brazil.

- **1889-1891** – Marshal Manuel Deodoro da Fonseca
- **1891-1894** – Marshal Floriano Vieira Peixoto
- **1894-1898** – Prudente José de Morais Barros
- **1898-1902** – Manuel Ferraz de Campos Sales
- **1902-1906** – Francisco de Paula Rodrigues Alves
- **1906-1909** – Afonso Augusto Moreira Penna
- **1909-1910** – Nilo Peçanha
- **1910-1914** – Marshal Hermes Rodrigues da Fonseca
- **1914-1918** – Wenceslau Brás Pereira Gomes / Rodrigues Alves (died before taking office)
- **1918-1919** – Delfim Moreira da Costa Ribeiro
- **1919-1922** – Epitácio da Silva Pessoa
- **1922-1926** – Arthur da Silva Bernardes
- **1926-1930** – Washington Luís Pereira de Sousa / Júlio Prestes (but wasn't the president because of the 1930 revolution)
- **1930** – Augusto Fragoso, Isaías de Noronha, Mena Barreto (temporary)
- **1930-1945** – Getúlio Dorneles Vargas
- **1946** – José Linhares (temporary)
- **1946-1951** – General Eurico Gaspar Dutra
- **1951-1954** – Getúlio Dorneles Vargas
- **1954-1955** – João Café Filho
- **1955-1956** – Carlos Luz, Nereu Ramos (temporary)
- **1956-1961** – Juscelino Kubitschek de Oliveira
- **1961** – Ranieri Mazzilli (temporary)
- **1961** – Jânio da Silva Quadros
- **1961-1964** – João Belchior Marques Goulart
- **1964** – Ranieri Mazzilli (temporary)
- **1964-1967** – Marshal Humberto de Alencar Castello Branco
- **1967-1969** – Marshal Arthur da Costa e Silva
- **1969-1974** – General Emílio Garrastazu Médici
- **1974-1979** – General Ernesto Geisel
- **1979-1985** – General João Baptista de Oliveira Figueiredo
- **1985** – Tancredo Neves (died before taking office)
- **1985-1990** – José Sarney
- **1990-1992** – Fernando Afonso Collor de Melo
- **1992-1995** – Itamar Augusto Cautiero Franco
- **1995-2002** – Fernando Henrique Cardoso
- **2003-2010** – Luiz Inácio "Lula" da Silva
- **since 2011** – Dilma Vana Rousseff

Interesting facts

- 3 presidents were teachers: Fernando Henrique Cardoso, José Sarney, and Jânio Quadros.
- 8 presidents were born in Minas Gerais: Afonso Penna, Wenceslau Brás, Delfim Moreira, Arthur Bernardes, Carlos Luz, Juscelino Kubitschek, Tancredo Neves, and Dilma Rousseff.
- Getúlio Vargas was president for 18 years, six months, and 19 days.

RESEARCH

1. How many presidents were born in the same state as you?

   ....

2. Which presidents were younger than 50 years old?

   ....
   ....

3. Who was the president in the year you were born? What do you know about him / her?

   ....

63

> ↑ **Road to success**
>
> **My English was, my English is**
> Como era o seu inglês há 2 anos? Você consegue perceber alguma evolução? Reveja os seus livros de inglês e cadernos dos anos anteriores. Você continua cometendo os mesmos erros de ortografia ou gramática?
> Essas comparações podem ajudar você a identificar erros recorrentes e a perceber padrões neles. Dessa forma, você poderá se concentrar em problemas específicos e fazer exercícios em livros e na internet ou pedir ajuda ao seu professor.

Speaking — Agreeing and disagreeing

1 Listen and read the dialogs. 🎧 22

Martha: Exercising used to be easier when I was younger.
Helen: That's so true.

better: comparative form of good

Lena: I think I look better with straight hair.
Maribel: I disagree. I love your curly hair!

worse: comparative form of bad

AGREEING	DISAGREEING
I agree.	I disagree.
That's so true.	I don't think so.
I guess so.	That's not true.
I'm with you on this.	No way.
You're right.	Not necessarily.

64

2 Talk to a partner. Give opinions about the topics below. Agree or disagree with his / her opinions and justify your opinions.
   a School was .... last year. (easier / more difficult / more interesting)
   b Music was .... in the 90s. (better / worse / more exciting)
   c I don't think .... (name of a soccer player) is a good player.
   d I think the food in the cafeteria is .... this year. (better / worse)
   e .... (name of a subject) is very easy!
   f I think .... (name of a celebrity) is awesome!

 **A class almanac**

Preparing to write
1. Decide what you want to write about to publish in a class almanac.
2. Make a list of sources you want to research (almanacs, encyclopedias, internet websites, etc.). Make sure you use reputable sources, such as government sites, well-known organizations, traditional newspapers and magazines, etc.
3. Underline the ideas you want to use.
4. Organize the ideas from different sources in a logical order to make a coherent text.

Draft
5. Rewrite the ideas using your own words. You can use parts of the original text. To do that, you need to use quotation marks ("") and credit the author.
   … like Mandela said, "A different world cannot be built by indifferent people."
6. Read your sentences again and double-check the information with the original text.
7. Proofread your text.

   Be careful: using three or more words from the original in a sequence is plagiarism too!

No plagiarism, please! **Plagiarism** is using a text (or work) from another person and not giving the credits. This is a crime. At school it can cause your suspension or expulsion.

Final version
8. Write a final version of your text.

Share
9. Put all the texts together and make a class almanac. Decide if you want to print it or publish it online.

   This activity was based on a guideline from page 36 in *National Geographic Kids Almanac 2010*, by National Geographic Society (U.S.), National Geographic.

Go to *Looking Back* on page 73 ▶ 65

Units 3 & 4

1 **Complete these sentences about technological problems. Then find the words in the grid.**

   a The computers at school always .... when we open lots of web pages!
   b I don't have a .... connection at home. I use a cable.
   c I get bad .... in my house with my cell phone.
   d To watch movies online you need a .... internet connection.
   e The cell phone .... is weak when you are in an elevator.
   f These machines .... on AAA batteries.
   g I want to listen to the radio, but the batteries are ....
   h I can save up to 4 MB of files in my .... drive.
   i This DVD player is not ....

A	H	P	D	K	T	S	E	V	A	R	R	Q	D	J
H	M	A	U	L	X	I	N	P	Y	Z	W	N	Z	N
H	E	N	V	C	X	G	I	T	C	S	A	T	D	B
D	L	W	D	S	N	N	Z	Q	U	B	K	B	B	J
F	R	O	N	Z	S	A	I	F	D	T	Q	H	J	N
X	U	R	Y	R	N	L	L	A	Y	N	H	Z	S	N
D	N	K	F	J	Z	X	O	U	Z	S	V	W	Z	B
O	O	I	L	O	G	R	L	Z	A	L	D	I	L	C
Y	P	N	A	H	B	W	I	R	D	V	Z	R	K	Q
I	A	G	S	V	U	M	C	I	Z	Q	O	E	Y	J
K	K	P	H	W	A	E	T	M	U	C	S	L	D	J
K	Z	Y	Y	C	T	S	L	E	O	A	K	E	E	E
G	O	W	U	C	P	R	L	P	T	K	J	S	K	H
R	E	C	E	P	T	I	O	N	J	Q	E	S	J	S
D	D	D	Y	Q	V	J	Z	Y	E	S	Q	A	Y	B

66 Units 3 & 4

2 Match the columns.

A
soccer shoes

◯ It used to be made of wood.

B
tennis racket

◯ They used to have fewer electronic components.

C
uniforms

◯ It used to be made by hand.

D
racing cars

◯ They used to be longer.

E
baseball

◯ They used to be heavier and harder.

3 Memory game

Student A: Look at the picture below for 1 minute and close your book.
Student B: Ask Student A questions about the photo using **was** or **were**.

B: Was the chair black?
A: Yes.

B: What was the time?
A: It was 10:10.

Stopover

Extra Reading 2

1 Can you imagine life before cell phones existed? What was different?

2 Read the text below and find out.

The World ALMANAC

Talking while on the move

It wasn't so long ago that you had two options if you needed to call someone: find a pay phone, or go home. Has your car broken down by the side of the road? Better start walking! But we have something today that has changed all of that, making our lives both safer and more convenient: the cellular radio telephone, or (as we call it today) cell phone. The cell phone was developed in the late 1970s. Even though the first ones were not very good, they were a great success. The reason is obvious: it's more convenient to make a phone call from wherever you are than to be forced to find a phone.

> **It's a fact!**
> New York is the first state to ban using hand-held cell phones while driving. In 2003, New York City became the first U.S. city to pass a law fining patrons of theaters and concerts for the use of cell phones during a performance.

By the mid 1990s cell phones were much better – and more and more people were using them. Cell phones help people to be safe, because having one means that you can call for help whenever and wherever you need it. Cell phones also make life more convenient. If you go to the supermarket and forget what your mother told you to buy, you can simply call her from the middle of the store. If you're driving to someone's house but can't find it, you can call and ask the person how to get there. Cell phones have even changed how people walk around, because you can be out for a walk in the California sun while talking to a friend who is looking at the New York skyline. And someone can call you on a cell phone, and reach you wherever you are. Cell phones make it easier for us to stay in touch with each other.

Nevertheless, all the news about cell phones is not positive. As cell phones have become more widely used in recent years, complaints about them have become more and more widespread – especially about their use in automobiles. Some recent studies seem to show that many serious accidents occur while drivers are talking on cell phones. The suggestion is that drivers are distracted by their conversations; the process of punching in a number; or by simply looking away from traffic to pick up the phone from a pocket, purse, or car seat. Less serious complaints come from patrons in restaurants and theaters who do not appreciate a nearby diner rudely carrying on a loud personal conversation at the next table or persons in theaters or concerts whose phones ring in the middle of performances. In fact, some cities have passed laws that fine people for the use of a cell phone under just such conditions as those mentioned above. It may be that the cell phone, like other technological achievements, is a double-edged sword. For all its many advantages, it seems that the cell phone is a mixed blessing – regarded by some as a great asset and by others as a public nuisance, or worse yet, as a threat to public safety.

MOORE, Greggory. *Take Five Minutes Fascinating Facts from the World Almanac.* Westminster, CA: Teacher Created Resources, 2004.

Glossary

blessing: something good that you feel very lucky to have

asset: a useful or valuable thing

nuisance: a person, thing, or situation that is irritating, offensive, obstructive, or dangerous

threat: the possibility of problem or danger

fining: punishing a person with the payment of money for doing something illegal

nevertheless: however, all the same

3 Read the text again and answer.
   a When was the cell phone invented?
   ....
   b What was the first American state to ban the use of cell phones while driving?
   ....
   c What are the problems that cell phones cause, according to the text?
   ....

4 Match.
   A. pocket   B. purse   C. seat   D. double-edged sword

5 In the text, find words that mean…
   a anywhere in all places; everywhere: ....
   b every time; any time: ....
   c distributed over a large area or number of people: ....
   d pressing (a button on a machine): ....

6 Why does the author say that the cell phone is a double-edged sword? INFER
....
....

YOUR TAKE

Do you think about manners when you use cell phones? What can you do to use your cell phone and respect other people? What is the appropriate way to use a cell phone in places such as movie theaters, restaurants and schools?

Extra Reading 2

Project 2

When I was 13...

1 What decade do you associate each image with?

1950s • 1960s • 1970s • 1980s

a first moon landing
....

b singer Elvis Presley
....

c Jovem Guarda
....

d Madonna
....

e champion of the Soccer world cup
....

f Isabel Martínez de Perón, president of Argentina ....

g singer Toni Tornado ....

h The constitution of Brazil ....

2 Match the photos above with sentences below.

In the world	In Brazil
◯ He used to be a rock 'n' roll idol of the 50s.	◯ Brazil was the winner of this 1958 event for the first time.
◯ Kids used to dream about becoming an astronaut, and Neil Armstrong was their idol.	◯ They were very popular with teenagers and young people of the 60s.
◯ She was the first woman to be head of government (non-monarch) in the Western Hemisphere.	◯ His performance of "BR-3" at the 5th International Song Festival was a surprise to the audience.
◯ She was a fashion icon in the 80s.	◯ It was a very important moment for democracy in Brazil.

3 Discuss your opinions about the life of teenagers in the past decades and make notes.

a What teens in the 50s used to do in their free time.
b What kind of music teens in the 60s used to listen to.
c What teens in the 70s used to wear.
d What teens in the 80s used to watch on TV.
e The most memorable moments for teens in the 90s.
f Teens' idols in the 00s.

4 Read the testimonials below. What decade do you think they are talking about?

When we were 13, there weren't many games or toys so we used to improvise. For example, we used to play war with castor beans on the street and when we were on the beach, we used to use the inner tube of a tire to float!

....

When I was 13, I was a big fan of music. But it was very hard to find information about new bands in Brazil, so I used to listen to a shortwave radio station from Britain. The sound was terrible, but I used to have a lot of fun!

....

When I was 13, I used to have long hair and very thick and long bangs (to hide my glasses). I used to wear rock T-shirts, mostly from Queen and Kiss, torn-at-the-knee jeans, and plastic high-heeled sandals.

....

5 Research. Interview five people who were teenagers in different decades. Talk to family members, friends, teachers, and neighbors and discover about their life when they were your age. Here are some suggestions of information to ask for during your interviews.
- Date of birth and what year it was when he / she was 13 years old.
- What teens in that decade used to wear, watch on TV, do in their free time, etc.
- The most memorable moments for teens in that decade.
- Their idols.

6 Write your interviews in the form of testimonials. Illustrate them with photos from the time and share with your classmates.

7 How was the life of teens in past decades different from your life now?

Glossary

use an inner tube of a tire to float

shortwave receiver

castor beans

Project 2 71

Looking Back at UNIT 1

Now I can...			Learn more about it:
read a sports webpage about Olympic sports and body types.			Watch the movie *Chariots of fire* (England, 1981), based on the real story of two British athletes who participated in the Paris Olympic Games in 1924.
describe physical appearance.			Find out what body type you have and what you should do to take care of it at <www.bodybuilding.com/fun/becker3.htm>.
read a text to learn more about the human skeleton.			Practice what you learned at <www.abcya.com/skeletal_system.htm>.
listen to a conversation about a physical evaluation.			
complete a medical evaluation form with personal information.			
contrast the verb *to be* and other verbs to talk about physical appearance and sports.			Study the information on page 140 in the *Grammar Reference* section.
pronounce the stop sounds.			
present a *show and tell* and introduce someone I admire to my classmates.			
reflect on my pace of learning to be more confident in my studies.			

Looking Back at UNIT 2

Now I can...			Learn more about it:
read an infograph about puberty.			Follow the blog *Daily infographic* to see everyday a new infograph. Available at <http://dailyinphografic.com/>.
talk about puberty issues.			Read more about it in the book *YOU: the owner's manual for teens: a guide to a healthy body and a happy life*, by Michael F. Roizen and Mehmet C. Oz.
use *should* or *shouldn't* to give advice.			
listen to a news report about puberty.			
use the comparative form of adjectives.			Study the information on page 141 in the *Grammar Reference* section.
read about how juggling can improve my coordination.			
identify British and American varieties.			Go to <http://accent.gmu.edu/browse_atlas.php> to hear native speakers of different countries reading the same text. You can participate too by recording yourself.
reflect on the effects of puberty in order to deal with it.			
write a message on an internet forum to get help.			

72   **Looking Back**

Looking Back at UNIT 3

Now I can...	😀 😕	Learn more about it:
read an advertisement about an old electronic device.		Take a look at more ads for old computers at <oldcomputers.net/oldads/old-computer-ads.html>.
talk about technology problems.		
talk about habits in the past with *used to*.		Study the information on page 142 in the *Grammar Reference* section. Learn the song *Used to*, by the band Daughtry, to practice the correct pronunciation of *used to*.
express doubt and disbelief to talk about old gadgets.		Study the information on page 142 in the *Grammar Reference* section.
read about bits and bytes to understand how the binary system works.		Learn how to write your name using binary: go to <www.durso.org/ynib/>.
use technology to learn English.		
listen to a customer calling a call center about product assistance.		
complete an online form to get support for a product.		

Looking Back at UNIT 4

Now I can...	😀 😕	Learn more about it:
read an almanac page about the 1990s.		Check the annual editions of the *The world almanac and book of facts*, published since 1868!
talk about almanac sections.		Visit <www.factmonster.com>, a free reference website for students, teachers, and parents.
use the verb *to be* in the past to talk about previous decades.		Study the information on page 143 in the *Grammar Reference* section.
ask questions in the past using the reduction of the verb *to be* and subject pronouns.		
listen to a TV game show.		Watch the movie *Quiz show* (EUA, 1994) and observe the backstage of a game show.
read about the presidents of Brazil to learn more about them and then do some research.		
reflect on the development of my English skills to focus on what I still need to improve.		
agree or disagree.		
write an entry to publish in a class almanac.		

Looking Back

73

Review Units 1 to 4

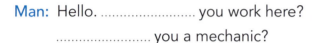

1 Complete the dialog below.

Man: Hello. ……………… you work here?
……………… you a mechanic?
Woman: Yes, I ………………. ……………… you need help?
Man: My car ……………… working. I think it ……………… the carburetor.
Woman: ……………… it make any sound?
Man: Yes, but it ……………… start.
Woman: OK. I have to open it to check.
(after some minutes)
Woman: It ……………… the carburetor.
Man: ……………… you know how to fix it?
Woman: Yes, you ……………… have to buy a new carburetor, just some new parts.
Man: ……………… they expensive?
Woman: No, they ………………. The sensor ……………… $50 and the thermostat ……………… $20.
Man: ……………… you accept credit cards?
Woman: ……………… it Crediclub?
Man: Yes.
Woman: ……………… sorry, we ……………… accept Crediclub.
Man: OK. ……………… National Bank near here?
Woman: Yes, it is. But you ……………… have to pay today.

2 Use the comparative form of the adjectives below and complete these sentences.

   strong • big • heavy • long • fast • small

a
The pincher ……………………… the chihuahua.

b
The blue egg ……………………… the yellow egg.
The red egg ……………………… the green egg.

74   Units 1 a 4

c  The red car .... the white car.

d  The daughter's hair .... the mother's.

e  The father .... the son.

3 Complete these sentences using *used to* and the past of *to be*.

a
She .... , now she is thin. Her diet .... very healthy.

b
This room .... , now it is red. It .... very boring, but now it is my favorite room in the house.

c
A: .... she a vegetarian last year?
B: No, she .... She .... , but not anymore.

d
This street .... It .... a residential area. Now it is very busy.

e
It .... the best turntable in the market. It .... very expensive too.

f
Boys and girls .... together in my school. We .... very good, but it .... fun.

Review 75

UNIT 5
Everyday mythology

Glory of Commerce, esculpido pela John Donnelly Company e concebido por Jules-Felix Coutan, 1914, Grand Central Terminal, Nova York, EUA.

ITINERARY

In this unit, you will develop the following competences:
- reading and answering a quiz to get general and specific information about the influence of mythology on our everyday lives;
- reflecting on beliefs about myths and facts and learning to identify them;
- learning adjectives to describe personality;
- using *there to be* in the past to talk about mythology;
- learning about etymology to understand the origin of some words;
- learning how to read phonetic transcriptions to understand dictionary entries;
- listening to a story to get general and specific information about the origin of *guaraná*;
- using expressions to ask for clarification;
- writing a review to give an opinion about a movie.

77

Reading

Quiz: how much do you know about the influence of mythology in our everyday life?

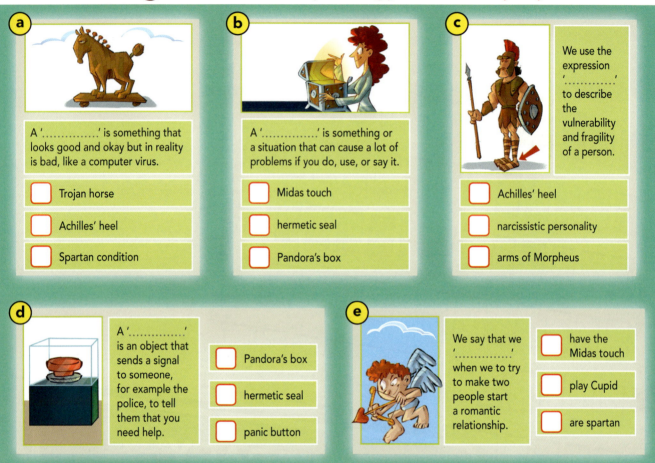

1 A *Trivia Quiz* is a kind of game in the form of a questionnaire. Complete the sentences with the words from the box. **GENRE**

answers   score   fun   titles   specific

a The objective of a **trivia quiz** is to test how much a person knows about a .... topic.
b Trivia quizzes have .... that usually appear in the form of a question, for example: "How much do you know about dinosaurs?"
c Trivia quiz questions have multiple-choice ....
d When you finish a trivia quiz, you calculate your .... and check how much you know about the topic.
e People like to answer trivia quizzes because they are .... and educational.

78

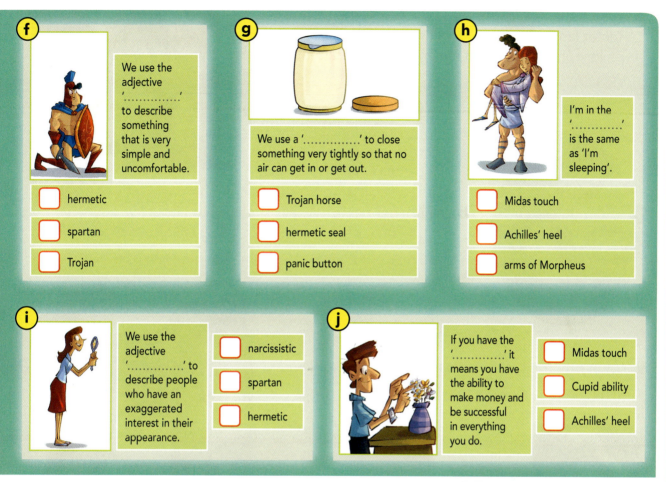

Check your score and read about the correct answers.

Glossary
Heel **Seal**

Answers
a. The Trojan Horse was a big wooden horse used by the Greeks to invade Troy during the Trojan war. The Trojans imagined it was a present, but the Greek soldiers were inside the horse.; b. Pandora was the first mortal woman who was curious about a jar and accidentally released all the things of humanity that are wrong or bad.; c. In Greek mythology Achilles was a hero that was invulnerable. Holding only his left heel, his mother dipped him into a magical river. That part of his body became his weakness.; d. In ancient Greece, Pan was the god of woods and of pastures. Pan was half man and half goat. The Romans called him Faunus. The word 'panic' comes from the terror caused by the god Pan.; e. Cupid is the god of desire in Roman mythology. He is a nude young boy that has wings and uses a bow and arrow. Golden arrows make people fall in love and lead arrows make people fall out of love.; f. Sparta was an ancient city in Greece famous for strict military discipline and a life without luxury.; g. The word hermetic is related to Hermes Trismegistus (the union of the Greek god Hermes and the Egyptian god Thoth), who used his knowledge in alchemy to magically seal boxes or chests so that it was impossible to open them.; h. Morpheus was the god of sleep and dreams.; i. In Greek mythology, Narcissus was a handsome young man who was in love with himself.; j. King Midas helped a satyr and the god Dionysus gave him the power to transform everything he touched into gold.

SCORE
0 to 5 points = MERE MORTAL: you know a little, but there is a lot to learn.
6 to 8 points = DEMIGOD: your knowledge is partly human, partly divine!
9 to 10 points = OLYMPIAN GOD: you are the source of all knowledge!

Unit 5 – Everyday mythology

79

2 Answer the questions based on the information from the quiz.

a Who is the man in this mosaic showing the Emerald Tablet (an artifact that contains a recipe for preparing the philosopher's stone that can transform metals into gold)?
....

b What's her name? What's she curious about?
....

c What's this? Inside this object there were soldiers. What nationality were they? ....

d Who's this? ....

e This is King Leonidas, holding a sword and a shield to represent his people's military discipline. What was Leonidas's nationality?
....

f What's the name of this king?
....

80

g What type of cupid arrow makes people fall in love?
....

Amour menaçant, de Étienne Maurice Falconet, 1755. Escultura em mármore. Museu do Louvre, Paris, França.

Honoré Daumier, O batismo de Aquiles. 1842, litografia, 25 x 19,5 cm. The Metropolitan Museum of Art, New York, EUA. Foto - © www.daumier-register.org

h Who are these people?
....

i Who is he?
....

Morfeu e Íris, de Pierre-Narcisse Guérin, 1811. Óleo sobre tela, 251 178 cm. Museu Hermitage, São Petersburgo, Rússia.

Narciso, de Michelangelo Merisi di Caravaggio, c. 1597-1599. Óleo sobre tela, 110 x 92 cm. Galeria Nacional de Arte antiga, Roma, Itália.

j What's his name?
....

↑ Road to success

Language Learning Myths

Existem muitos mitos sobre o aprendizado de um idioma:

"**Basta aprender uma quantidade grande de palavras para aprender um idioma.**" Um idioma não é feito apenas de palavras, mas também da relação lógica entre elas ou das frases entre si. Assim, você precisa aprender a usar essas palavras em combinações coerentes.

"**Um professor nativo é melhor.**" Isso só é verdade quando o professor é qualificado e experiente. Falar um idioma e ensiná-lo são habilidades diferentes.

"**A melhor maneira de aprender um idioma é viver em um país onde a língua é falada.**" Sem dúvida, a necessidade de se comunicar e enfrentar o dia a dia em outro país é um grande incentivo, mas você precisa de alguém qualificado para ajudá-lo a entender a cultura e os costumes daquele país.

Faça uma lista das coisas nas quais você acredita com relação a aprender um novo idioma. Converse a respeito com o seu professor e aprenda a separar os mitos dos fatos.

Unit 5 – Everyday mythology

81

Vocabulary — Talking about personality

1 Listen and read the dialog. Underline the adjectives to describe personality. 🎧23

Man: Who's that?
Woman: That is Achilles. He was the Greek hero of the Trojan War.
Man: What was he like?
Woman: He was intelligent, proud, and temperamental.

2 Distribute the adjectives from the box into the categories below. Use a dictionary if necessary. Then listen and check your work. 🎧24

> annoying • cheerful • curious • dull • easygoing • friendly • intelligent • reliable • rude • selfish • sensitive • serious • shy • stubborn

Positive	Negative	Neutral
....	....	....
....	....	....
....	....	....
....	....	....
....	....	....

3 Ask your classmate.
  a What's your best friend like?
  ....
  b What's your mother like?
  ....
  c What's your favorite teacher like?
  ....
  d What are your neighbors like?
  ....
  e What are you like?
  ....

4 Find an adjective to describe your personality that starts with the first letter from your name and create a new nickname for you. Use the dictionary, if necessary.

Friendly **F**abiana
Shy **S**heila

....
....
....
....

82

Grammar — There to be – past

1 Read.

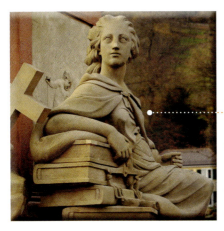

There were many Roman festivals dedicated to specific gods. The ancient Romans believed that gods lived everywhere, even under our beds!
There was a temple dedicated to the goddess Minerva in Rome.
There weren't strong female figures in Irish mythology.
There wasn't a written African language until the 8th and 9th centuries. Before that, the stories of African mythology were only verbal.

2 Answer.

a What's the past of **there is / there isn't**?
   ○ there was / there wasn't
   ○ there were / there weren't

b What's the past of **there are / there aren't**?
   ○ there was / there wasn't
   ○ there were / there weren't

> In the interrogative form, we invert the position of words. Note:
> **Was there** a statue of Zeus on Mount Olympus?
> **Were there** mythological characters half man and half horse?

3 Read about the Guaraní people and their mythology and complete the blanks with the past of *there to be*.

Before the Europeans arrived in South America, ... a large group of indigenous people living here: the Guaranís.
In Guaraní mythology, ... a god of creation called Tupã. .... also a moon goddess, Arasy, who helped Tupã create the ocean, forests, and animals.
.... many monsters in Guaraní mythology. The most important were Teju Jagua, god or spirit of caverns and fruits; Mbói Tu'ĩ, god of water and aquatic creatures; Moñái, god of the open fields; Ao Ao, god of hills and mountains; and Luison, god of death.
.... (negative) any written records of Guaraní mythology in the past. .... (negative) a Guaraní language until modern times, so the entirety of their religious beliefs was passed verbally from generation to generation. Because of that, there are different stories of various gods, myths, and legends, depending on the region.

Adapted from en.Wikipedia.org

167

Unit 5 – Everyday mythology

83

Crossroads: Languages — English

Etymology

Where do words come from? Why do many languages have the same or similar words for the same things? Finding answers to these questions is the responsibility of etymologists. Etymologists study etymology, which is the study of the history of words, their origins, and how their form and meaning changes.

1 Where do you think these words are from? How old do you think they are?

jaguar   banana   safari
avatar   iceberg   ketchup
karaoke   zero   golf

2 To find the correct answers in an etymology dictionary, you need to know how to read the entries. Read the example and write the missing information.

armadillo 1570s, from Spanish *armadillo*, diminutive of *armado*, "armored".

a word: ....
b approximate date it appeared in the English laguage: ....
c origin: ....
d meaning of the word in the original language: ....

3 Read these entries from an etymology dictionary and check your guesses in activity 1.

jaguar big cat of the Americas (*Felis onca*), c.1600, from Tupi *jaguara*, said to be a name "denoting any larger beast of prey."
avatar 1784, from Skt. *avatarana* "descent" (of a deity to the earth in incarnate form).
karaoke 1979, from Japanese, from *kara* "empty" + *oke* "orchestra".
banana 1590s, from a W. African word, possibly Wolof, *banana*.
iceberg 1774, partial loan-transl. of Du. *ijsberg*, lit. "ice mountain," from *ijs* "ice" + *berg* "mountain."
zero c.1600, from It. *zero*, from M.L. *zephirum*, from Arabic *sifr* "cipher," translation of Skt. *sunya-m* "empty place, desert, naught."
safari 1890, from Swahili, lit. "journey, expedition," from Arabic, lit. "referring to a journey," from *safar* "journey."
ketchup 1711, from Malay *kichap*, from Chinese (Amoy dialect) *koechiap* "brine of fish."
golf mid-15c., Scottish *gouf*, usually taken as an alteration of Du. *colf*, *colve* "stick, club, bat."

Glossary

c.: circa (approximate date)
mid-15c: middle of the 15th century (1450-approximate date)
Skt.: Sanskrit, the classical Indian language
wo lof: a language spoken in African countries like Senegal, Gambia, and Mauritania
Du.: Dutch, the language of Holland
It.: Italian
M.L.: Medieval Latin, c.700-c.1500
swahili: an African language spoken in many countries
malay: the official language of Malaysia, Indonesia, Brunei, and Singapore

Pronunciation — Pronunciation in a dictionary

You can use the dictionary to learn pronunciation too. You can check the stress of the word, the syllabic division, and the correct way to pronounce these syllables. For example, let's look at the word **safari**:

This symbol shows the stress of the word and it appears before the stressed syllable. In some dictionaries the symbol can be a little different.

/səˈfari/

safari: noun (countable) /səˈfari/ a journey, especially to Africa, in order to watch or take pictures of wild animals.

1 Look at the phonetic transcriptions below and underline the stressed syllable.
saf<u>a</u>ri /səˈfari/
  a ketchup /ˈketʃəp/
  b reliable /rɪˈlaɪəbəl/
  c avatar /ˈævəˌtar/
  d temperamental /ˌtempərəˈmentəl/
  e intelligent /ɪnˈtelɪdʒənt/

2 Listen and check. Practice the pronunciation of the words. 🎧 25

Listening — Storytelling

Storytelling is the ancient tradition of telling stories.

1 Write T (True) or F (False). GENRE
  a ◯ Storytelling was present only in European cultures.
  b ◯ The objectives of storytelling are to entertain, to educate, to preserve the culture and to pass on moral values.
  c ◯ The elements of storytelling are the events of the story, characters, and methods to tell the story.
  d ◯ During the course of history, oral stories like tales and legends were memorized and then passed from generation to generation.
  e ◯ Storytelling is not common nowadays.

2 Listen and choose the appropriate title. 🎧 26 SKIM
  ◯ The importance of *guaraná* for indians
  ◯ The origin of *guaraná*
  ◯ The medicinal uses of *guaraná*

3 Listen again and order the story. 🎧 26 SCAN
  ◯ *Guaraná* is born.
  ◯ Tupã wants the parents to plant the child's eyes to create a new plant.
  ◯ Tupã gives the boy to the couple.
  ◯ An indian couple asks Tupã for a baby.
  ◯ Everybody in the village likes the boy.
  ◯ Jurupari transforms into a snake and attacks the boy.
  ◯ Jurupari decides to kill the boy.

Unit 5 – Everyday mythology

85

Asking for clarification

1 Listen and read. 🎧 27

> A: <u>Look before you leap?</u> <u>I'm not sure I understand what you mean.</u>
>
> B: I mean you should check your possibilities before making a decision.
>
> A: Oh, I get it now.
>
> A: Hmm… I still don't get it. I'll look it up in a dictionary.

Other ways to ask for clarification
The meaning is not very clear to me.
What are you trying to say?
What does that mean?

2 Work with a partner. Follow the instructions below.

a Student A: Ask Student B to clarify the meaning of the proverbs below.
Student B: Go to page 149.

> The grass is always greener on the other side.
>
> No pain, no gain.
>
> Birds of a feather flock together.

b Student A: Now, clarify Student B's doubts.

> **Too many cooks spoil the broth**: where there are too many people trying to do something, there's confusion.
>
> **Better safe than sorry**: you should be careful. If you aren't, you can regret it.
>
> **When in Rome, do as the Romans do**: when you visit a different place, it's better to respect the local customs.

3 Work in pairs and discuss: do you agree with the messages of these proverbs? Justify your opinions and if you don't understand your friend's opinion, ask for clarification.

WRITING

Movie review

Preparing to write

1. Research movies that include mythology or legends. Choose one to watch and write a review about it.

Draft

2. Write the topics to include in your review, for example: title, director, main actors, movie plot (a short description of the story – but don't tell the end!), your opinion (Do you recommend the movie or not? Justify.).
3. Write the information for each topic.
4. Transform your notes above into a text. Don't use topics this time. Write all the information in complete sentences and group the sentences into paragraphs.
5. Proofread your text.

Proofreading TIP

Repetition makes your text uninteresting and tiring. To avoid it, use a **thesaurus**, which is a dictionary of synonyms and antonyms. Just keep in mind that not all synonyms are appropriate to all the contexts. So before you use a synonym, look it up in an English-English dictionary or ask the help of your teacher. Practice with this movie review:
• First, underline the repeating words.

"The movie *Percy Jackson: The Lightning Thief* is excellent. It is very exciting, and the effects are excellent too.
Percy Jackson is a common teenager. He has a terrible stepfather that is very bad to Percy and his mother. But one day Percy finds out that he is special. He is the son of Poseidon. Percy is accused of stealing Zeus' lightning bolt, and that can cause a terrible war between the gods. Another terrible thing happens: Hades, God of the Underworld, takes Percy's mother because he wants the lightning bolt too. Percy goes to the underworld to save his mother.
The only problem is that the story is excellent, but it is very different from the book by Rick Riordan."

• Read the thesaurus entries and replace the repeating words in the review.

excellent /ˈeksələnt/ adj
Synonyms: wonderful, exceptional, first-class, notable, outstanding
Antonyms: bad, imperfect, inferior

terrible /ˈterəbəl/ adj
Synonyms: bad, horrible, awful, unpleasant
Antonyms: good, great, nice

Final version

6. Write a final version of your text and check for repetition of words.

Share

7. Put all the reviews together and publish a magazine of movie reviews. You can share your magazine with other classes that are studying mythologies.

Go to *Looking Back* on page 136 ▶ 87

Unit 5 – Everyday mythology

UNIT 6
The young and talented

ITINERARY

In this unit, you will develop the following competences:
- reading a DVD blurb to get general and specific information about a movie;
- learning words to describe professions;
- reading a text to discuss emotional intelligence;
- using expressions to show surprise;
- understanding the concept of syllables;
- learning the superlative form of adjectives to make comparisons;
- writing a comment to reply to a post;
- listening to a newscast to get general and specific information about a child prodigy.

 A DVD blurb

1. A blurb is a short description of a book, movie, or other product written and used for promotional purposes and printed on the outside of something (outside a DVD case, for example). Which information do you usually find in a film blurb? **GENRE**

   - ○ opinions from movie critics
   - ○ the movie script
   - ○ awards
   - ○ interview with actors
   - ○ production credits
   - ○ special content (extras, director's cut, deleted scenes, etc.)
   - ○ the minimum age for which the content is appropriate

2. Read the blurb extract below and answer: What kind of movie is it? **SKIM**

   - ○ comedy
   - ○ drama
   - ○ adventure
   - ○ terror

His talent made him unique.
His heart made him normal.

Switzerland's official 2006 Academy Awards® entry, official selection of the Berlin Film Festival, and winner of the AFI Film Festival Audience Award, *Vitus* is the story of a child prodigy who has everything he wants – except the chance to be a normal kid.

At six, Vitus is both incredibly talented and wonderfully precocious. When it becomes evident that he has an exceptionally high IQ and can play piano like a young Mozart, expectations run high. His parents love him, his grandfather understands him, but no one knows the truth – that his real genius in his heart.

Glossary

Switzerland: a country in Europe
IQ: abbreviation for intelligence quotient
Mozart: Wolfgang Amadeus Mozart, Austrian composer and child prodigy
award: prize
truth: the quality of being true

3 Read the blurb again and answer. SCAN

   a What country is this film from?
   ....
   b Who is Vitus?
   ....
   c How old is Vitus?
   ....
   d What instrument does he play?
   ....
   e Is he intelligent?
   ....
   f Why is he precocious?
   ....

YOUR TAKE

What are the advantages and disadvantages of being a child prodigy?
....
....
....
....
....
....

Vocabulary Professions

1 Read about these other child prodigies and complete the sentences with the professions from the box. Then listen and ckeck your work. 🎧18

author • computer system administrator • artist • lawyer • piano and cello player • doctor

Marc Yu is a ....
He was 7 years old when he received the Davidson Fellows Scholarship award, a financial help for extraordinary young people under the age of 18.

Adora Svitak is the world's youngest teacher and ....
At the age of 6, she was famous for her writing abilities.

Haris Imtiyaz Khan was only 10 in 2010 when he was able to draw a live portrait in 30 seconds. He is the youngest live portrait .... of the world.

In 2007, at the age of 18, Kathleen Holtz was the youngest .... in America. She entered the University of California School of Law at the age of 15.

Balamurali Ambati was the world's youngest .... in 1995. At the age of 17, he graduated from Mt. Sinai School of Medicine.

Marko Calasan, from Macedonia, is the youngest certified .... in the world. He was 8 when he passed an exam with Microsoft!

92

2 Match these other jobs with the professionals. Then listen and ckeck your work. 🎧29

- ○ waiter / waitress
- ○ doorkeeper
- ○ systems analyst
- ○ hairdresser
- ○ housekeeper
- ○ police officer
- ○ businessperson
- ○ cook
- ○ construction worker
- ○ engineer

3 Write sentences about these people and their jobs. Use a dictionary, if necessary.

> mother • father • neighbor • aunt • uncle • best friend

My father is a Spanish teacher and my mother is a dressmaker.

1. ....
2. ....
3. ....
4. ....

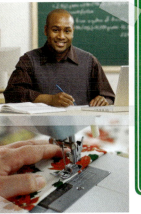

EQ

Prodigies have a natural ability to do something extremely well, but does that mean they will be successful in the future?

1 In your opinion, what is necessary to be successful in the future? Justify.
- ○ Come from a traditional family.
- ○ Have money.
- ○ Be motivated.
- ○ Understand other people's emotions.
- ○ Have the ability to control your emotions.
- ○ Other: ....

2 What do you know about emotional intelligence? Read about it and check your expectations.

Emotional Intelligence – EQ

Emotional Intelligence (EQ) is a theory that says that success requires more than IQ. We all know people who are academically brilliant but are socially and interpersonally inept. And we know that a high IQ does not guarantee success.

According to the EQ theory, the competencies and skills you need to have to be successful are
1. Know your emotions.
2. Manage your emotions.
3. Motivate yourself.
4. Recognize and understand other people's emotions.
5. Manage relationships, i.e., manage the emotions of others.

When we develop these competencies and skills, we can become more productive and successful at what we do and help others to be more productive and successful too. Emotional Intelligence development also reduces stress for individuals and organizations, by decreasing conflict, improving relationships and understanding, and increasing stability, continuity, and harmony.

Adapted from: BusinessBalls.com

3 According to the text, which items from **activity 1** are necessary to be successful?
....
....
....

4 According to the text, can your social status determine your future success? Justify. **INFER**
....
....

YOUR TAKE

1. In your opinion, do you have good EQ? Why (not)?
....

2. What can you do to improve your EQ?
....

Speaking   Showing surprise

1 Listen and read. 🎧30

A: Justin Bieber is an autodidact. He learned to play the piano, drums, guitar, and the trumpet without help.
B: I can't believe it!

Other expressions
No kidding!
Are you for real?
Come on!
That blows my mind.

2 Work in pairs. Follow the instructions below.

a Student A: Read the sentences below to Student B.
Student B: Go to page 150.

| Dean Karnazes can run 50 marathons in 50 days. | Jessica Tandy was the oldest Oscar winner, at the age of 80, for *Driving Miss Daisy*. |
| Robert Pershing Wadlow was the tallest man in history. He was 2.72 meters high. | Tatum O'Neal was the youngest Oscar winner, at the age of 10, for *Paper Moon*. |

b Student A: Now listen to the facts Student B reads and react.

3 Think about some information about yourself that your classmates probably don't know. Tell four different classmates about your "thing".

Pronunciation   Syllables & rhythm

The rhythms of Portuguese and English are very different. Portuguese rhythm is based on syllables, and English rhythm is based on stress.

In English, words have fewer syllables than they seem to have for Brazilians. The word **house**, for example, has one syllable, and **chocolate** has only two. This happens because many written vowels are not pronounced in English. In Portuguese, on the contrary, we have a tendency of adding vowels in oral language ("*adevogado*", "*pissicólogo*").

1 Listen and repeat. Pay attention to the sounds of the syllables. 🎧31
ONE SYLLABLE: young, fast, fine
TWO SYLLABLES: qui-et, hap-py, sil-ly, ug-ly, heal-thy, wor-ried, la-zy, mod-ern
THREE SYLLABLES: ex-pen-sive, im-por-tant, de-ter-mined, suc-cess-ful
FOUR SYLLABLES: en-er-get-ic

Grammar: Superlative form

She is **the youngest** musician of the orchestra, but she is not **the most experienced**.

1 Read the photo caption and answer the questions.

  a What's the sentence comparing?
  ○ Two people.
  ○ The members of a group.

  b In the first sentence, we use **the + adjective + ...** and in the second sentence we use .... **+ adjective**.

  c What's your conclusion? Complete with **short** or **long**.
  To make superlatives, we use **the most** when the adjective is a .... word and we use **-est** when the adjective is a .... word.

Short adjectives have one syllable and sometimes two syllables, if the adjective ends in -y, like **easy**. Long adjectives have two or more syllables.

2 Write the adjectives in the correct column.

> young • happy • fast • expensive • quiet • important • silly • ugly • fine • talented • determined • energetic • healthy • worried • lazy • modern • successful • tired • fat

Short adjectives	Long adjectives
....	....
....	....
....	....

3 Read and complete the spelling rules for short adjectives.
  a This is the **biggest** change in my career.
  b He was the **funniest** person in the world to me.
  c This is the **largest** classroom in the school.

  For adjectives ending in **consonant, vowel, consonant**, we double the last .... + **-est** to form the superlative. Another adjective that follows this rule is ....

  For adjectives ending in **-y**, we remove the y and include .... to form the superlative. Another adjective that follows this rule is ....

  For adjectives ending in **-e**, we only include .... to form the comparative. Another adjective that follows this rule is ....

96

EXCEPTIONS The following adjectives have irregular forms:
good → **the best**   bad → **the worst**   far → **the furthest**

4 Complete this dialog with the superlatives.

Melvin: This is .... show in the history of rock 'n roll! (good)
Vanessa: I don't know if it is the best, but I'm sure it is ....! (large) Look at that stage!
Melvin: Yeah, but we have .... seats in the stadium! (bad) I can't see it well from here!
Vanessa: Well, they were .... tickets. (cheap) These were .... seats available. (close)
Melvin: $ 150 is the cheapest? How much were ....? (expensive)
Vanessa: $ 900!
Melvin: Wow!

5 Write sentences about 5 classmates using the superlative form.
1. André is the most intelligent student in our class.
2. ....
3. ....
4. ....
5. ....
6. ....

YOUR TAKE

"It is not the strongest of the species that survives, nor the most intelligent, but the one most responsive to change." (Charles Darwin)
Do you agree with Darwin?

....
....
....

Unit 6 – The young and talented

97

WRITING Replying to a post

HOME | **CATEGORIES**

discussion forum!

Ask [_____] Go

My Top 10 Animated Movies

Posted by **@rmadiLLO** on November 29, 2011 at 3:PM in Teen Talk Too.

Here's my list of the BEST ANIMATED MOVIES. What do you think of it? If you think a movie is missing from this list, post a link to me at the bottom! Luv yall!

My Top 10 list: Animated Movies
1. *Shrek* (2001)
2. *Rio* (2011)
3. *Madagascar* (2005)
4. *Over the Hedge* (2006)
5. *The Chipmunk Adventure* (1987)
6. *Chicken Run* (2000)
7. *Bambi* (1942)
8. *All Dogs Go to Heaven* (1989)
9. *Ratatouille* (2007)
10. *Bolt* (2008)

Comments on My Top 10 Animated Movies

DudeToon on November 30, 2011, 3:39 PM

Wow, great list. But the best animated movie OF ALL TIMES in my opinion is Wall-E (2008) (*^_^*) and I don't agree with Bolt in this list. That was booooriiiiing LOL!

JanethRXY on November 30, 2011, 6:04 PM

I agree. :-) Wall-E is the best animated movie. But Shrek is SOOOOO GOOOOOD! Hmm... what about Kung Fu Panda? It's the funniest movie in my opinion! :D

Preparing to write

1. Read the post and the comments on the top 10 animated movies.
2. Do you agree with @rmadiLLO's list?
3. Do you agree with the comments?

Draft

4. Write a comment to @rmadiLLO's post. Mention your opinion about his list, say what you agree and disagree with, and explain why.
5. Include your name (or nickname), the date, and the time you are writing your comment.
6. Proofread your text.

Final version

7. Get a strip of paper with your teacher.
8. Write the final version of your comment on the strip of paper.

Share

9. Post your comment on the board. The comments on a blog are ordered from top to bottom, from oldest to newest. Check where your post should go.
10. After all your classmates have posted their comments, read them and write replies if you want to comment on a post your classmates wrote.

Proofreading

A text should be appropriate to its media. An internet forum, for example, tends to be an informal environment. That's why it's OK to use abbreviations, emoticons, capital letters in the middle of the sentences, etc.

Listening — A newscast

1 A newscast is a news program. What do you know about newscasts? [GENRE] Write the words in the correct place.

> elements • interview • pictures • one to five • reports • presenter

Newscasts are always introduced by a news .... The presenter reads *links* and introduces the news reporter. Most news stories are live or .... recorded previously, usually with the duration of .... minutes. News reporters collect and edit .... clips, ... , and their script to tell a story. They record a *voice-over* to explain the pictures and connect all the ....

2 Listen to a TV newscast about a child prodigy and answer: (32) [SKIM] what's Alejandro's special talent?

- ◯ He can memorize anything he reads or anything you read to him.
- ◯ He can read and speak very fast.

3 Listen again. Check the information that is mentioned. (32) [SCAN]

- ◯ Alejandro is 7 years old.
- ◯ Alejandro is from California.
- ◯ Alejandro can remember all the capital cities of the world and all the names of the American presidents.
- ◯ Carlos and Muriel are Alejandro's parents.
- ◯ Alejandro has a sister.
- ◯ Alejandro memorized the 1970 Brazilian National soccer team.

Unit 6 – The young and talented

Go to *Looking Back* on page 136 ▶ **99**

Stopover Units 5 & 6

1 Help the Minotaur out of the maze, collect the words, and find out the secret sentence.

Maze words: THE, CRETE, BULL, HALF, THE, LIVED, THESEUS, MAZE, HEAD, A, HORRIBLE, IN, LEGEND, OLD, ISLAND, OF, GREECE, ON, MINOUTAUR

Secret sentence:
....

2 Unscramble the words and find out the first professions of these celebrities.

a Lady Gaga used to be a **T S A I R W E S**. ....

b Beyoncé used to work with her mother as a **S I E R R A S H E R D**. ....

c Sheryl Crow was an elementary school **H E C T A R E**.
....

100   Units 5 & 6

d Matthew McConaughey was a **I N C U R S C O T T O N E R R W O K** in Australia. ....

e Mick Jagger was a **R A D O N O M** at a mental hospital. ....

f Andrea Bocelli was a **A W R E L Y**. ....

3 General knowledge quiz.

a The longest highway in the world is the Trans-Canada.
○ true ○ false

b Everest is the highest mountain in the world.
○ true ○ false

c The Sahara is the biggest desert in the world.
○ true ○ false

d The official coldest temperature on Earth was recorded in Vostok, Antarctica at −89.2 °C.
○ true ○ false

e Agha Jari, in Iran, is the hottest place in the world, with a temperature of 53.33 °C
○ true ○ false

f At the first modern Olympic Games there were no female competitors.
○ true ○ false

g There wasn't a full moon on February 1865.
○ true ○ false

h The oldest tree in the world is located in California and is more than 4,830 years old.
○ true ○ false

i There were no cats on the Titanic.
○ true ○ false

j There were 32 teams at the 2002 FIFA World Cup.
○ true ○ false

SCORE
0-3: Weak. You need to read more!
4-7: Good. But you can do better!
8-10: Excellent. Congratulations!

Stopover
101

Extra Reading 3

1 Look at the movie poster and answer.
  a What kind of movie is it?
  b Who are the main characters?
  c In your opinion, is this movie appropriate for children? Why?

2 Read and check your answers in activity 1.

From the studio that brought you *Shrek*, *Madagascar*, and *Kung Fu Panda* comes this adventure comedy set in the mythical world of burly Vikings and wild fire-breathing dragons, based on the book by Cressida Cowell.

The story centers around a Viking teenager named Hiccup, who lives on the Island of Berk, where fighting dragons is a way of life. The teen's rather progressive views and offbeat sense of humor don't sit too well with his tribe or its chief, who just happens to be Hiccup's father, Stoick the Vast.

When Hiccup is included in Dragon Training with the other Viking teens, Astrid, Snotlout, and Fishlegs, he sees his chance to prove he has what it takes to be a fighter. But when he encounters (and ultimately befriends) an injured dragon, his world is flipped upside down, and it turns into an opportunity to set a new course for the future of the entire tribe.

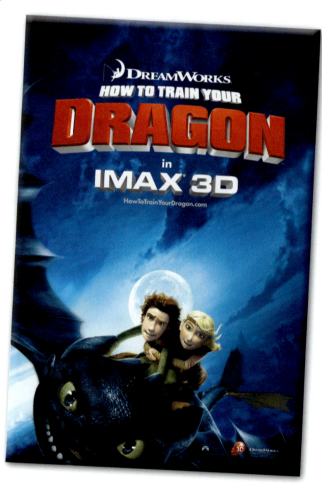

Adapted from HowToTrainYourDragon.com

3 Read the text again and answer.

a What is the connection between this movie and *Shrek*, *Madagascar*, and *Kung Fu Panda*?

....

b Who wrote the book that the movie is based on?

....

c Who is the chief of the tribe?

....

4 Match the words and definitions.

a burly ⃝ A person or animal that fights, like a soldier.

b wild ⃝ To have a physical problem caused by violence or accident.

c set in ⃝ Unconventional.

d offbeat ⃝ Lifestyle.

e fighter ⃝ Not domesticated.

f befriend ⃝ Become friends with.

g a way of life ⃝ Large and strong.

h injured ⃝ Complete; all.

i entire ⃝ To display a movie at a specified time or in a specific place.

5 What are the meaning of these expressions?

a don't sit well ....

b happens to be ....

c to have what it takes ....

d flipped upside down ....

YOUR TAKE

Which information in this text is important for your decision to watch it or not? Why?

....

....

....

Extra Reading 3

103

Project 3

Quiz Show

A quiz show (or game show) is a type of television program where participants play a game which involves answering questions or solving puzzles. The players compete alone or in a team. The winners receive prizes such as cash, trips and products, and services provided by the show's commercial sponsor.

1 Do you watch quiz / game shows? How many quiz / game shows can you name?
....
....

2 Let's prepare a quiz show to play in class.
  a Decide what topics your group is going to make questions about. Choose at least 3 topics.
   ○ mythology   ○ etymology
   ○ records   ○ celebrities
   ○ TV and movies   ○ others: ....

  b Prepare the questions and research the correct answers. You can use the information you learned in Units 5 and 6 or your own ideas. Give three options of answers. Here are some examples of questions:

  Who was the oldest Oscar winner?
  a) Jessica Tandy at 80.
  b) Dean Karnazes at 90.
  c) Tatum O'Neal at 78.
  Who was Tupã in Guarani mythology?
  a) The god of the moon.
  b) The god of the sun.
  c) The god of creation.

  c Write each question on a separate card, include the answers and mark the correct one.

104   Units 5 & 6

3 A quiz show needs a presenter. What is a TV presenter like?

  a List some characteristics that you think a quiz show presenter needs to have.

  ....
  ....
  ....
  ....
  ....
  ....
  ....
  ....
  ....

  b Organize a class election to choose the person in the class who has these (or some of these characteristics) to be the quiz show presenter.

4 A quiz show also needs a sponsor. Who should be the sponsor of your show?

  a You can think of a real company or an imaginary one. Give your opinion and justify it. Then, decide with your classmates on the best sponsor.

  ....
  ....

  b The sponsor is responsible for providing the prize. What is the prize of your quiz show?

  ....
  ....

5 Give your quiz show a name! Be creative!

  ....
  ....

6 Time for the show! Organize the classroom and present your TV quiz show. Ask your teacher or someone from another classroom to be the cameraman to record the show!

Project 3

Black Power

ITINERARY

In this unit, you will develop the following competences:
- reading an article to learn more about the Black Power movement;
- learning words to talk about what people are wearing;
- using expressions to give and respond to compliments;
- using relative pronouns to talk about influential African-Brazilian artists;
- reading about and listening to some African instruments to learn more about music;
- developing strategies to use music to learn English;
- practicing the sounds of the letter "i" to pronounce some words;
- listening to a school presentation to get general and specific information about the Viscount of Jequitinhonha;
- preparing and presenting a speech about an African-Brazilian you admire.

Reading

Black Power: much more than a haircut

1 Do you know the movement called "Black Power"? What do you think it is? Read and check.

Black Power was a movement which made history between the end of the 70s and beginning of the 80s. Its objective was to make people assume their identity and be proud of their blackness. The higher your hair was, the more respected you were.

Much more than a hair style, black power was a way to encourage African-Brazilians to discuss the prejudice, racism and social inequality that always tormented them.

Hair salons were meeting points for black men and women and a place to show beauty, arts, ideas, and pride, things that would change the behavior of African-Brazilians in the future.

The first Brazilian celebrity to assume the style was Toni Tornado, followed by Tim Maia and Zezé Mota. The Black Power hair was a symbol of modernity and even white people adopted the look.

Fashion was also an important part of the Black Power movement. African-Brazilians used to wear hats, glasses, high-waist trousers, short jackets, and platform shoes. Clothes were colorful and extravagant and they represented the originality and authenticity of the young black people of that time.

■ Tim Maia

■ Toni Tornado

■ Zezé Mota

Translated and adapted from "Black Power – a força negra". *Raça* magazine. (RacaBrasil.uol.com.br), Africanidades.com

2 Answer the questions.

a According to the text, why was "Black Power" more than a hair style?

....

....

b What was the relation between hair and respect?

....

c Who else adopted the Black Power hair?

....

d Why were clothes colorful and extravagant?

....

....

3 Match the words from the text with their meaning.

a pride   ◯ feeling happy or showing respect for yourself
b proud   ◯ the feeling of being proud
c behavior   ◯ related to the African-Brazilian culture
d look   ◯ an opinion formed with limited information
e blackness   ◯ the quality of not being equal
f prejudice   ◯ the manner you interact with people and the environment
g inequality   ◯ appearance

YOUR TAKE

In your opinion, how can African-Brazilians demonstrate that they are proud of themselves?

....

....

Stokely Carmichael (1941-1998) was a civil rights activist and national chairman of the Student Nonviolent Coordinating Committee who created the term "Black Power" in 1966.

From Wikipedia.org

Unit 7 – Black Power

Vocabulary Clothes

1 Read and listen.

110

2 Answer the questions about the families.

a This is the Rodrigues family: Jair Rodrigues, his son Jair Oliveira, and his daughter Luciana Mello. Jair Rodrigues and his children are famous Brazilian musicians.

- What's Jair Oliveira wearing?
  He's wearing a black jacket.
  ....
- What's Luciana wearing?
  ....
- What's Jair Rodrigues wearing?
  ....

b This is the Pitanga family. Antonio Pitanga, Vera Manhães (*in blue*) and their two children: their daughter Camila and their son Rocco, who are actors. Benedita da Silva is Antonio's wife. She was the governor of Rio de Janeiro.

- What's Camila wearing?
  ....
- What's Antonio wearing?
  ....
- What's Rocco wearing?
  ....
- What's Vera wearing?
  ....

c This is Isabel Fillardis' family. Isabel (*the third woman from left to right*) is a Brazilian model and actress. The others in the photo are her husband Júlio César, her mother Sônia, her sister Jaqueline, and her daughter Analuz. The one in white is singer Márcio Victor.

- What's Júlio César wearing?
  ....
- What's Sônia wearing?
  ....
- What's Isabel wearing?
  ....

3 Answer.

a What are you wearing today?
....

b What's your teacher wearing today?
....

Unit 7 – Black Power

111

 Giving and responding to compliments

1 Listen and read. 🎧 34

Amelia: I like your hair! It looks good on you.
Marie: I'm glad you like it.

Chris: Nice sneakers!
Drew: Thanks. They were a present from my father.

Giving compliments
- Nice earrings!
- Those are cool sneakers you are wearing!
  That's a nice T-shirt you are wearing!
- I like your hair.
- Nice cap! It looks good on you.
  Nice shoes! They look good on you.
- You look good in green.

Responding to a compliment
- I appreciate that.
- Thanks for noticing.
- Thank you.
- I'm glad you like it.

2 Go around the classroom and give a compliment to some of your classmates. When you receive a compliment, respond appropriately. Remember: a real compliment has to be honest and show true admiration.

A false compliment is called *flattery*.
It is not sincere and it has the intention of getting something you want.

Grammar

Relative pronouns – *who, which, that*

James Brown was a singer <u>who</u> influenced a lot of Brazilian artists.

"The Godfather of Soul" is the nickname <u>which</u> he received.

> **That** can substitute both words:
> James Brown was a singer **that** influenced a lot of Brazilian artists.
> "The Godfather of Soul" is the nickname **that** he received.

1 Choose the correct answer.

  a The word **who** is related to…

  ◯ a person.   ◯ an object or thing.

  b The word **which** is related to…

  ◯ a person.   ◯ an object or thing.

2 Complete this description with **who** or **which**.

Soul music is a style of music ………………… combines gospel, rock and roll, and rhythm and blues.

Tim Maia, Hyldon, Cassiano, Jorge Benjor, Banda Black Rio, and Wilson Simonal are some artists ………………… represent Brazilian soul music.

A Onda é o Boogaloo (1969), by Eduardo Araújo, is the record ………………… is considered the first soul music record of Brazil.

The first record ………………… Tim Maia released was in 1970.

Jorge Ben and Wilson Simonal were artists ………………… used to mix soul music and Brazilian rhythms.

Toni Tornado, ………………… is more famous today as an actor, started his career as a singer. Nowadays, Ed Motta, Luciana Mello, and Simoninha are examples of artists ………………… continue the tradition of Brazilian soul music.

Unit 7 – Black Power

Music | Crossroads | English

African instruments

The Africans who arrived in Brazil in the 1500s contributed to the development of Brazilian music. There are many instruments which have an African origin, and they are used in religious ceremonies and music such as samba, *maracatu*, *axé*, etc. But can you recognize their sounds?

1 Listen and match the instrument to the sound.

Sound 1 ◯   Sound 2 ◯   Sound 3 ◯   Sound 4 ◯
Sound 5 ◯   Sound 6 ◯   Sound 7 ◯

a. djembe
b. kalimba
c. afoxé
d. berimbau
e. caxixi
f. udu pot
g. agogo

2 Do you know how these instruments are played? **INFER**

↑ Road to success

Learning English with music

Nós nos lembrarmos mais facilmente das palavras quando elas estão inseridas em um contexto musical. Isso acontece porque a música nos emociona. Além disso, a estrutura em que as informações são apresentadas, sejam palavras ou frases, facilita a memorização e a reprodução. Veja algumas sugestões para aprender inglês por meio da música:

1. Decore as letras de suas canções favoritas.
2. Preste atenção às frases e palavras utilizadas, assim como ao ritmo das sentenças e ao modo como os sons das palavras se conectam.
3. Antes de ler a letra de uma música, tente identificar algumas palavras. Esse é um ótimo exercício para desenvolver suas habilidades de escuta.
4. Cante! Isso vai ajudar você a desenvolver a pronúncia e a articulação dos sons.

Pronunciation — The sounds of the letter *i*

1 Look at these words from this unit. Check how the letter *i* is pronounced in each word.

| /ɜ/ like in skirt | /aɪ/ like in tie | /ɪ/ like in Brazil | /ə/ like in pencil |

2 Listen to the words below and divide them into the correct sounds of the letter *i*. 🎧 36

COUSIN   WHITE   SHIRT   RIGHT
PREJUDICE   ARTIST   KIND
FIRST   LIKE   AFRICAN   ORIGIN

/ɜ/ skirt	/aɪ/ tie	/ɪ/ Brazil	/ə/ pencil
....	....	....	....
....	....	....	....

Listening — An oral presentation

1 Jasmine's teacher asks the class to research about an important person in the History of Brazil. She decides to talk about Francisco Jê Acaiaba de Montezuma, Viscount of Jequitinhonha. Do you know what a Viscount is?

2 What is true about this man? 🎧 37
- ○ He is the only African-Brazilian viscount.
- ○ He was the first president of Brazil.
- ○ He was the first president of the Institute of Lawyers of Brazil.
- ○ His real name was Francisco Gomes Brandão.
- ○ He was the son of an Aztec emperor.
- ○ He was important for the independence of Brazil.
- ○ He was an important politician.

Unit 7 – Black Power

Writing & Speaking

A speech about an African-Brazilian I admire

Preparing your speech

1. What important African-Brazilian person in the history of Brazil would you like to talk about? This person can be an athlete, an artist, a politician, someone you know, etc.
2. Why do you admire him/her? Research about this person's life: where and when he/she was born, what his/her profession is/was, what he/she is/was like, what he/she is/was famous for etc.

Draft

3. Using your research, write some notes about the person. Include the information you researched and the reason why you admire him/her. These notes will help you talk about the person later.
4. Proofread your text. Remember to avoid plagiarism and repetition. (See the Writing sections of Units 4 and 5.)

Proofreading TIP

When you write in topics, make the items parallel. Look at the two examples:

Some important facts of his life were the following:
- In 1955 Martin Luther King Jr. receives Doctorate of Philosophy in Theology
- He visited India in 1959 to study Gandhi's philosophy of nonviolence
- In 1962 King goes to prison
- Time Magazine elected him Man of the year In 1964

Some important facts of Martin Luther King Jr.'s life were the following:
- In 1955 he receives Doctorate of Philosophy in Theology;
- In 1959 he visits India to study Gandhi's philosophy of nonviolence;
- In 1962 he goes to prison;
- In 1964 he is on the cover of Time Magazine as Man of the Year.

The second list is easier to read because all the sentences have a parallel structure.

Final version

5. Use your notes to prepare a slide show to help you with your oral presentation to the class.When you prepare a slide show, remember to do the following:
   - Use the layout to make something attractive.
   - Communicate with simplicity. You are not going to read the slides; they are your guide only.

- Don't write too much on one slide. Slide shows are not pieces of "readings" for the audience! They are meant to keep the audience's attention and concentration on you.
- Use images to illustrate what you are talking about.
- Use transitions and animations but not too much. They are the element of surprise; if you overuse them, they are not interesting anymore.

Share

6. Go back to Unit 1 (page 22) and revise the steps in making a presentation.
7. Use your research and the slide show to help you in the presentation.

When you talk to a crowd, remember the following:

1. **Relax.** You are ready. You have prepared for this, so there is no need to be worried. You know the material and you know your audience.
2. **Find a place for your hands.** Moving hands distract an audience. One hand in your pocket can look okay, but both hands in your pockets looks bad. Hold papers (calmly) in one hand by your side, but don't wave them around.
3. **Smile.** A smile on your face will make your audience respond more positively to you. It will also help you feel better.
4. **Use appropriate humor.** If you use a joke to open your speech, make sure it's a good one. It should be funny without offending anyone.
5. **Share your enthusiasm.** You are speaking about a subject you know. You are prepared. You are relaxed and smiling. Use this presentation as a way to share your enthusiasm with your audience and it will be a fine presentation.

Adapted from Management.about.com

8. Present it to your classmates and listen to their presentations. Did you know the people in your classmates' texts? What's interesting about them?

Go to *Looking Back* on page 137 ▶

UNIT 8 Homemade gifts

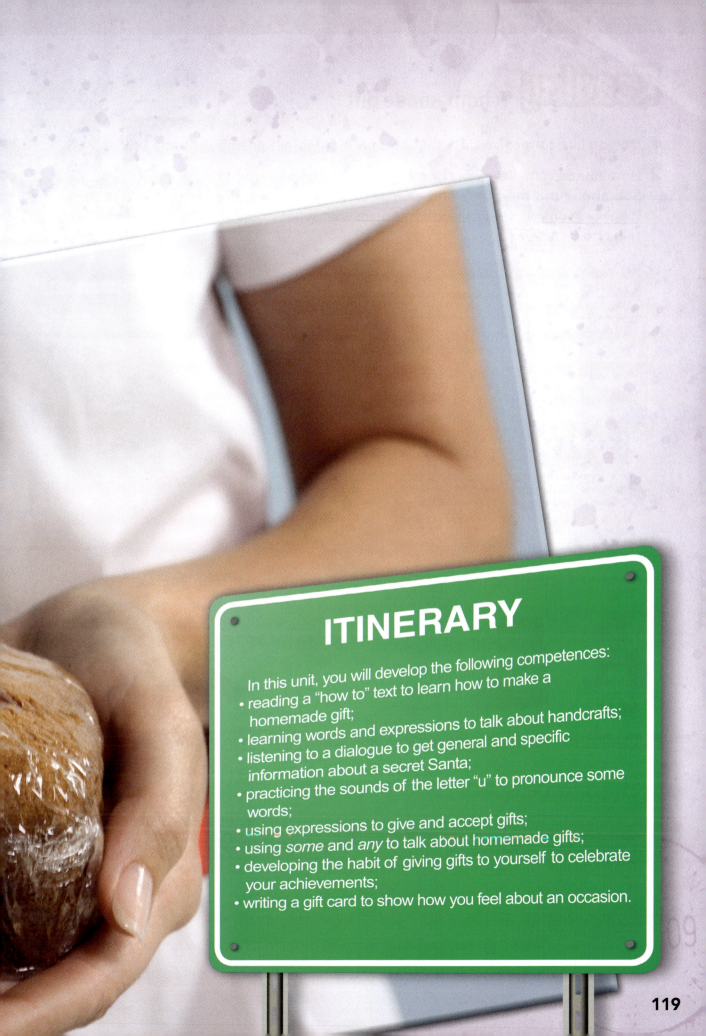

ITINERARY

In this unit, you will develop the following competences:
- reading a "how to" text to learn how to make a homemade gift;
- learning words and expressions to talk about handcrafts;
- listening to a dialogue to get general and specific information about a secret Santa;
- practicing the sounds of the letter "u" to pronounce some words;
- using expressions to give and accept gifts;
- using *some* and *any* to talk about homemade gifts;
- developing the habit of giving gifts to yourself to celebrate your achievements;
- writing a gift card to show how you feel about an occasion.

Reading A homemade gift

1 Do you like to receive gifts that are made at home, not bought at a store? Why?

2 Homemade gifts are great because they are meaningful and personal. Somebody put their time and energy to think about it, preparing it and making it special for you. Read the text and answer: what homemade gift does the text talk about? SKIM

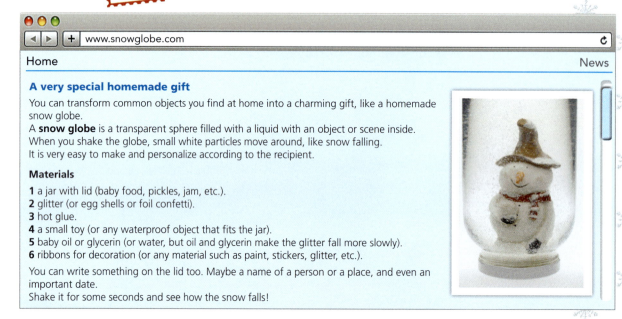

www.snowglobe.com

Home   News

A very special homemade gift

You can transform common objects you find at home into a charming gift, like a homemade snow globe.
A **snow globe** is a transparent sphere filled with a liquid with an object or scene inside. When you shake the globe, small white particles move around, like snow falling.
It is very easy to make and personalize according to the recipient.

Materials

1 a jar with lid (baby food, pickles, jam, etc.).
2 glitter (or egg shells or foil confetti).
3 hot glue.
4 a small toy (or any waterproof object that fits the jar).
5 baby oil or glycerin (or water, but oil and glycerin make the glitter fall more slowly).
6 ribbons for decoration (or any material such as paint, stickers, glitter, etc.).

You can write something on the lid too. Maybe a name of a person or a place, and even an important date.
Shake it for some seconds and see how the snow falls!

3 Match the images to the material mentioned in the text (from 1 to 6).

4 The instructions were removed from the text. Put them in order.

(1) Remove the label and clean your jar to remove any residue. It has to be totally clean and transparent.

( ) Decorate the lid with ribbons, paint, paper, or any other materials you have available. Your homemade snow globe is ready! Shake it and enjoy it!

( ) Fill the jar with some baby oil (or water with glycerin). Remember – the level of the liquid rises with the toy; so don't fill it up completely.

( ) Use some hot glue to fix the toy to the inside of the jar lid.

( ) Add the "snow" (glitter, broken eggshells, or foil confetti). Do not exaggerate.

( ) Apply glue to the lid to hermetically seal the jar. Wait until it is completely dry.

Vocabulary   Handcraft

1 Match the object to its use. Then listen to check your work. 🎧38

a scissors   **b** scotch tape   **c** glue stick   **d** paper cutter (box cutter)

e brushes   **f** Styrofoam   **g** gouache paints

to make models — to paint — to glue — to cut — to tape

2 Choose which paper you use when you want to do the activities below. Then listen and check your answers. 🎧39

cardboard — foil paper — crepe paper — printing paper
cellophane — wrapping paper — colored paper — Kraft paper

a make a card
....

b wrap a present
....

c print school research
....

d decorate a party
....

e wrap a flower bouquet
....

f fold an origami
....

g use as draft paper
....

Unit 8 –Homemade gifts

121

3 Use the words from activities 1 and 2 to complete the texts.

A scrapbook is a decorated album containing photos, text, and decoration. To make a scrapbook page we need .... , ... , ... , ... , one sheet of .... , markers (or colored pens), buttons and ribbons of different colors. First we .... some pieces of wrapping paper and some pieces of colored paper. Then we organize the papers and the decoration on the cardboard. After that, we .... everything on the cardboard, write something about the occasion, and include a photograph.

To make a piñata you need some candy, one balloon, ... , ... , ... , ... , and .... First you need to fill the balloon with the candy and blow it up. Then, ... small pieces of crepe paper and .... them around the balloon. Use a paper cutter to make cones of Styrofoam and glue the cones around the balloon (and form a star). Use the cellophane (or foil) and the crepe paper to decorate the cones. If you want, you can also .... the piñata using different colors of gouache paints.

Paper is produced using cellulose, which is a fiber that comes from wood. That means we have to cut down trees to produce paper. So use paper responsibly: write on both sides, use scraps as draft paper, and never throw out old paper – recycle it.

122

Geography Crossroads English

Gift traditions around the world

1 Can you identify these countries by their flags and the descriptions below? Complete the text with the name of each country.

 In ...., people avoid clocks and the number **four** when they give gifts because these words have a similar sound to the word **dead** in their language.

 It is impolite to open gifts immediately in .... You should wait until your guests leave your house.

 At a baptism in ...., each guest receives a *boubouniera* (an almond covered with sugar). The candy represents the sweetness of the future life, and the almond represents the bitterness.

 In ...., you have to bring a box of sweets, called mithai, or dried fruits when you visit your friends and family on special occasions.

It is very important to give a thank-you gift when you are invited to someone's house in .... Appropriate gifts are flowers, candy, or liquor.

 If you are invited to visit someone's home in ...., don't bring chrysanthemums. They are associated with funerals.

 In ...., close friends expect gifts from you when you return from a trip or holiday.

 In ...., people give bread and salt to family members or friends when they move into a new house.

 In ...., people send hand-written 'thank you' cards, usually in the same week that they received the gifts.

When you go to a wedding in ...., the tradition says that you have to give golden coins to the bride, worth a hundred or more dollars, to put on her dress.

2 Which of these countries' traditions are similar to Brazilian traditions?
....

3 Why is it important to know and understand other countries' different traditions?
....
....
....
....
....
....

4 Do you know the traditions and correct etiquette for giving gifts in Brazil? Answer the questions about them.

a When do Brazilians give gifts?
....
....

b In Brazil, what is considered an appropriate gift for…
- a friend on his / her birthday?
....
- an older family member on his/her wedding anniversary?
....
- your teacher on Teacher's Day?
....
- a secret Santa?
....
- a friend's family member you don't know very well?
....

5 Does your family have any gift-giving tradition?
....
....
....
....

 The colors of the Olympic rings are blue, yellow, black, green, and red. At least one of these colors is present on the flag of every country in the world.

124

Listening · Secret Santa

1 Read the text and answer: do you know any variations of this tradition?

Secret Santa is a popular Christmas tradition among groups of friends at work or school and even family members. They write the names of the participants on pieces of paper, and everybody picks a name. They can't tell each other who they picked, and everybody buys anonymous gifts.
On a pre-determined day, the gifts are placed on the same table or in a room. When it's time to exchange gifts, everybody has to find their gift and guess who their Secret Santa is.
Sometimes the participants write a list of presents they would like to get, but usually there is a price limit.

2 Listen and complete the chart below. 🎧40

Number of participants	....
Price limit	....
Date for gift exchange	....

3 Listen again and write B for a boy, or G for a girl. 🎧40

a ◯ Who writes the names?

b ◯ Who suggests the price limit of $30?

c ◯ Who gets the first paper in the first round?

d ◯ Who gets her/his name and they have to start over?

e ◯ Who gets the first paper in the second round?

f ◯ Who suggests the date for the gift exchange?

g ◯ Who doesn't wear green?

4 What kind of relationship do the four people have? Are they close or distant friends? Explain. **INFER**

YOUR TAKE

In the end, one of the girls says they shouldn't give each other gift certificates because they are too impersonal. Do you agree with her? Explain.

....

....

Unit 8 – Homemade gifts

125

Pronunciation — The sounds of the letter *u*

1 Look at these words from this unit. Check how the letter *u* is pronounced in each word.

- /u/ like in incl**u**de
- /ʌ/ like in c**u**p
- /ɜ/ like in ret**u**rn
- /ʊ/ like in p**u**t
- /ə/ like in **u**ntil
- /ju/ like in **u**se

1 Listen to the groups of words. Cross out the one that is different from the others. 🎧 41

a future – cut – USA – usually
b such – cutter – cut – furniture
c suggest – music – success
d number – Russian – funeral – brushes

Speaking — Giving and accepting gifts

1 Listen and read. 🎧 42

Pamela: Here, this is for you!
Amy: That's so kind of you!

Jackie: Surprise!
Karina: Wow! Cool! Thanks!

Giving gifts
- Here, this is for you!
- Surprise!
- Here, I hope you like it!

Accepting gifts
- Wow! Cool! Thanks!
- That's so kind of you! Thank you!
- Oh, thanks, you shouldn't have!

2 Get together in groups of four students. Draw a gift for everybody in your group on separate pieces of paper. Fold the papers and exchange the gifts with the people in your group.

Grammar *Some* and *any* – countable vs. uncountable

1 Read the paragraph and underline the correct options.

A HOMEMADE BOOKMARK – A GREAT GIFT IDEA

Do you need any ideas for a gift for a friend? Why not a personalized bookmark? To make bookmarks, you need scissors or a paper cutter, some cardboard paper, some stickers, some photos (real or from magazines), and some glue. If you don't have any stickers or photos, you can use some paint or markers and make drawings. You can also use some glitter and some ribbons to decorate your bookmarks.

a We use *some* in *affirmative / negative / interrogative* sentences.

b We use *any* in *affirmative / negative / interrogative* sentences.

c The words *stickers*, *photos*, *markers*, and *ribbons* are in the *singular / plural* because you *can / can't* count them. We call these words countable nouns.

d The words *paper*, *glue*, *paint*, and *glitter* are in the *singular / plural* because you *can / can't* count them, we need to refer to the separate parts (examples: sheet of paper, glue tube, etc). We call these words uncountable nouns.

e We don't use *a-an-the / some-any* with countable nouns.

Unit 8 – Homemade gifts

127

2 Complete the dialog with *some* or *any*.

Amy: It's grandma's birthday next week. Do you have .... gift suggestions?
Eric: We can make her a memo pad.
Amy: Great idea! What do we need?
Eric: We need a photo frame, ... colored paper, scissors, ... paint, and a notepad.
Amy: Do we need .... glue?
Eric: Oh, yes, sure. .... glue. And .... stickers too.
Amy: I don't think we have .... stickers, let's go buy ....

3 Complete the instructions with *a*, *an*, *some*, or *any*.

Cakes in .... cup

Make two cakes: .... orange one and .... chocolate one. Both cakes need to be rectangular and have the same size. Cut your cakes in 10 pieces. Wrap each the pieces of cake in .... cellophane. Close each piece of cake with .... ribbon. Put one piece of each cake in .... cup and add .... personalized card. If you want, you can decorate each cake with .... granulated chocolate or .... sugar before you wrap it. Don't use .... cream on the top; it will be difficult to wrap!

↑ Road to success

A gift for yourself

É importante comemorar suas conquistas. Se você se esforçou para conseguir uma boa nota em uma prova, por que não dar a si mesmo um presente? Pode ser um pôster para pendurar em seu quarto para lembrá-lo da conquista; um almoço especial para marcar a ocasião; um dia de folga para fazer as coisas de que você mais gosta etc.
Caso seu objetivo seja a longo prazo, você pode dividi-lo em etapas e determinar presentes ou comemorações para cada etapa superada.
Além de servir de motivação extra, esse reconhecimento vai ajudar você a aumentar sua autoestima.

Writing   A gift card

If you are giving a present, you probably want to write a personalized gift card that shows how you feel about the recipient or the occasion (birthday, Christmas, wedding, etc). If you want the recipient to appreciate your gift, take some time to write a personalized message. It is better than copying a message from the Internet.

Preparing to write
1. Choose an appropriate card for the occasion.
2. Think about a salutation to open your message with. You can use the traditional "To my dear friend", or mention a funny nickname or memory that you have together.
3. Think about a personal message that expresses how you feel about the occasion, the gift, or your relationship with the person.

Draft
4. Start with the salutation, then the message. In the end, identify yourself with a signature.
5. Proofread your text.

Proofreading TIP
Take a break between writing and proofreading. Sometimes even five minutes of distance from your text can help you see problems or mistakes and find the solutions.

Final version
6. Write the final version of your gift card.
7. Remember to write your name on the envelope before you put it with the gift.

Share
8. Give your gift to your friend.

Go to *Looking Back* on page 137 ▶ **129**

Unit 8 – Homemade gifts

Units 7 & 8

1 Can you find these clothing items?

> T-shirt • shirt • jeans • sweater • shorts • tank top • shoes • dress • skirt • pants

2 Secret message. Unscramble the words related to handcraft and copy the letters in the numbered boxes to find out the secret message.

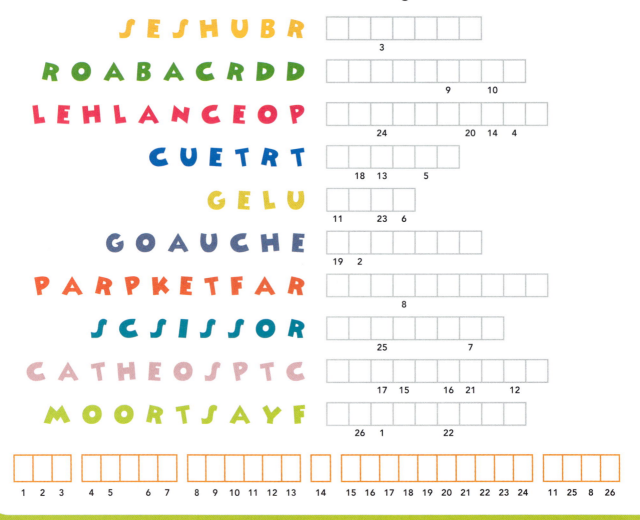

3 Crosswords.

African-Brazilian celebrities

Across (→)

6. (1958-): Former Brazilian Presidential candidate and Minister of Environment.

9. (1942-): first black female Governor in Brazil.

10. (1976-): singer, Artist of the year award at the Billboard Latin Music Award 2001.

Down (↓)

1. (1975-): considered to be the best fighter in the history of MMA (Mixed Martial Arts).

2. (1959-): comedian, member of Casseta & Planeta.

3. (1926-2001): geographer famous for his works in various fields in geography.

4. (1962-): singer, nominated for a Grammy Award in the categories "Best World Music album" and "Best Brazilian Contemporary Pop Album".

5. (1970-): singer and reality show judge.

7. (1954-): Minister of the Supreme Court of Justice.

8. (1853-1905): pharmacist, journalist, writer, orator and political activist.

Stopover

Extra Reading 4

1 Look at the band's photo and name and answer.
  a What kind of music do you think this band play?
  b Is it a Brazilian band?

2 Read and check your answers in activity 1.

http://itunes.apple.com/au/album/id324917040

Banda Black Rio

MARIA FUMAÇA (1977)

ALBUM REVIEW

This is the CD reissue of the opening LP by Banda Black Rio, recorded in 1977. The instrumental band, dissolved in 1980, had an excellent work of electric samba-funk fusion, with hot brass arrangements, a good percussive section, and good solos. This first album brings the hit "Maria Fumaça," included in the homonymous soap opera. The album also has good performances of Luiz Gonzaga's "Baião," Edu Lobo's "Casa Forte," and Ary Barroso's "Na Baixa do Sapateiro," along with the band's originals.

BIOGRAPHY

The Banda Black Rio was formed in 1976 by the late Oberdan (Oberdan Magalhães). Characterized by a sound in which rhythm & blues served as the vehicle for danceable variations incorporating the gafieira style, samba, and jazz, the band had in its variable formation, the trumpeter José Carlos Barroso, drummer Luís Carlos dos Santos, keyboardist Jorge Valdir Barreto, guitarist Cláudio Stevenson Jorge, and bassist Valdecir Ney Machado, among others. Their first hit was the

samba-funk "Maria Fumaça," released in the eponymous LP (WEA, 1977). The song was the theme of the soap opera Loco-Motivas (TV Globo). Recording originals and versions for songs like "Na Baixa do Sapateiro" (Ary Barroso) and "Casa Forte" (Edu Lobo), they were compared in the specialized press to other soul-funk bands like Kool and the Gang and Earth, Wind and Fire, having success in England's dance houses in the late '90s. The band recorded two more LPs — Gafieira Universal (RCA,1978) and Saci Pererê (RCA 1980) — until 1980, when they dissolved. In 1999, the Banda Black Rio resumed activities with a new formation led by Oberdan's son William Magalhães.

From itunes.apple.com

3 **Read the text again and answer.**
  a When was Banda Black Rio formed?

....

  b Who was the creator of Banda Black Rio?

....

  c What was the name of Banda Black Rio's first album?

....

  d When was the band a success in England's dance houses?

....

  e How many albums are mentioned?

....

  f Who is the leader of Banda Black Rio's new formation?

....

4 **Match the words and definitions.**

  a reissue
  b brass
  c homonymous
  d soap opera
  e along with
  f late
  g eponymous

  ◯ that have the same name
  ◯ in the company of
  ◯ a new version of the CD
  ◯ a person who is no longer alive
  ◯ a dramatic serial TV program
  ◯ something that gives its name to something
  ◯ the section of a band or orchestra that plays instruments like trumpets, horns, trombones

YOUR TAKE

What is important for you when you choose a CD to listen to? Rank these items from 1 (very important) to 5 (not very important). Justify your answers.
(   ) CD cover.
(   ) Name of the songs.
(   ) Photos.
(   ) Review.
(   ) Biography.

Extra Reading 4   133

Project 4

Designing a new school uniform

1 Is there an official uniform in the school where you study? Do you like it?

....

2 In your opinion, what are the advantages and disadvantages of having a school uniform?

....

....

3 School uniforms are very different from one country to another. Do you know what uniforms are like in other parts of the world? Match the pictures with the descriptions.

a Ghana

b Malaysia

c Indonesia

d Pakistan

e Cuba

○ Boys wear white shirts with red shorts and girls wear red skirts and white shirts. Boys and girls wear red ties.

○ Twelve and thirteen-year-old girls wear the *shalwar kameez*, a traditional unisex dress that is similar to a very long shirt with pants.

○ All children have to wear uniforms there. The uniforms are brown and orange and very thin (because the weather is very hot).

○ School uniforms are used by all children there. A blue scarf is part of the school uniform for boys and girls.

○ All children who go to public schools have to wear uniforms there. Girls wear navy blue dresses and white shirts and boys wear navy blue pants and white shirts.

- Which of these is your favorite uniform? Why?

....

....

134 Units 7 & 8

4 School uniforms also change from time to time. How do you compare the school uniforms from the past with the ones we have now?

....

....

5 In your opinion what are the characteristics of a good school uniform?

- ○ It's comfortable.
- ○ It's fashionable.
- ○ It's colorful.
- ○ It's traditional.
- ○ It's informal/casual.
- ○ It's discrete.
- ○ It's different for boys and girls.
- ○ It's the same for boys and girls.
- ○ It's cheap.
- ○ It's resistant (you can wear the same uniform for 2 or 3 years).
- ○ It has many different pieces to make different combinations.
- ○ It doesn't have many pieces, only the necessary ones.
- ○ Others? ....

6 Let's design a new uniform for your school.

a What pieces are there in the new uniform?

....

b What are the colors of your new school uniform?

....

7 Most school uniforms have the school name and logo printed on the T-shirt. Copy the T-shirts models below on a sheet of paper to draw where the logo of the school is on the new uniform.

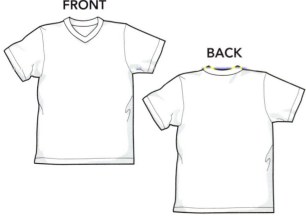

FRONT

BACK

8 On a separate sheet of paper, draw a clothesline with the pieces of your new school uniform.

9 Present your designs to the class. Use your answers from Activities 6 to 8 in the presentation. Here's an example to help you:

This is our design for the new school uniform. It's a fashionable, casual, and cheap uniform. It's the same for boys and girls and it doesn't have many pieces, only the necessary ones. The T-shirt is light blue and orange, the jacket and pants are dark blue…
The school logo appears on the top front of the T-shirt…

 Why not use your design as a real suggestion? Find out who is responsible for choosing the uniform design in your school (the principal, the government) and send your suggestion.
Maybe they will like your design!

Project 4

Looking Back at UNIT 5

Now I can...	😀	😕	Learn more about it:
read and answer a quiz about the influence of mythology on our everyday lives.			Answer other quizzes at <http://quizilla.teennick.com/hubs/trivia-quizzes>.
reflect on beliefs about myths and facts and learn to identify them.			Read more about mythology in *Oh my Gods!: a look-it-up guide to the Gods of mythology* (Mythlopedia).
describe personalities.			
use *there to be* in the past to talk about mythology.			Study the information on page 144 in the *Grammar Reference* section.
learn about etymology to understand the origin of some words.			Check the history and evolution of more than 3,000 words at <www.etymonline.com>.
read phonetic transcriptions to understand dictionary entries.			
listen to a story about the origin of *guaraná*.			Watch some episodes of the series *Are you afraid of the dark?*, which tells the story of teenagers who get together to share horror stories. Available at <www.imdb.com/title/tt0103352>.
ask for clarification.			
write a review to give an opinion about a movie.			

Looking Back at UNIT 6

Now I can...	😀	😕	Learn more about it:
read a DVD blurb.			
describe professions.			
read a text to discuss emotional intelligence.			Read *People smarts for teens: becoming emotionally intelligent*, by Carol Carter.
use expressions to show surprise.			
understand the concept of syllables.			
use the superlative form of adjectives.			Study the information on page 145 in the *Grammar Reference* section.
write a comment to reply to a post.			
listen to a newscast about a child prodigy.			

136   **Looking Back**

Looking Back at UNIT 7

Now I can...	😊 😟	Learn more about it:
read an article about the Black Power movement.		Watch the short film *Vista a minha pele* (Brasil, 2004), by Joel Zito Araújo and Dandara, a parody on the reality of the Brazilian racial scenario. Find it on YouTube.com.
talk about what people are wearing.		Surf the Internet for fashion and style websites. Some suggestions: <www.gq.com/style> for boys and <www.polyvore.com> for girls.
give and respond to compliments.		
use relative pronouns to talk about influential African-Brazilian artists.		Study the information on page 146 in the *Grammar Reference* section.
read about and listen to some African instruments to learn more about music.		Know the best African music at <www.afropop.org/radio/streams.php>. Also, watch the documentary *Throw down your heart* (2008, EUA), which shows the travels of a banjo player in Africa, as he searches for the origin of the instrument.
use music to learn English.		
produce the sounds of the letter *i* to pronounce some words.		
listen to a school presentation about the Viscount of Jequitinhonha		
prepare and present a speech about an African-Brazilian I admire.		

Looking Back at UNIT 8

Now I can...	😊 😟	Learn more about it:
read a "how to" text to learn how to make a homemade gift.		Find other ideas for homemade gifts in the book *The best craft book ever*, from DK Children, 2006.
talk about handcrafts.		
listen to a dialog about a secret Santa.		
produce the sounds of the letter *u* to pronounce some words.		
use expressions to give and accept gifts.		
use *some* and *any* to talk about homemade gifts.		Study the information on page 147 in the *Grammar Reference* section.
give gifts to myself to celebrate my achievements.		
write a gift card to show how I feel about an occasion.		

Looking Back 137

Review  Units 5 to 8

1 **Complete this conversation about the ship SS *Thistlegorm* with the past of *there (to be)*.**

Liam: What are these photos?

Joseph: They are from my diving expedition.

Liam: Oh, really? What is this ship?

Joseph: This was the SS *Thistlegorm*. It was a British military supply ship that was bombarded by the German army on October 6th, 1941, during World War II. Jacques Cousteau rediscovered it in 1955.

Liam: .... anything important in it?

Joseph: Well, ... motorbikes and jeeps in it. And .... a locomotive too!

Liam: Wow... wait, ... boots in the ship?

Joseph: Yes. .... many things there, but they are disintegrating fast.

Liam: .... skeletons in the ship?

Joseph: No, ...! But there were 32 survivors.

Liam: How do you know all this information?

Joseph: .... a guide in the expedition and he was very talkative.

2 **Complete the dialogs with the superlative form of the adjectives in parentheses.**

a

Man: Is this .... model? (powerful)

Salesman: No. But it is .... and .... model. (modern / light)

Man: I believe it is .... too, right? (expensive)

Salesman: Well, it is not ...., but we have .... price in the city! (cheap / good)

138   Units 5 to 8

b Grandson: What are you doing, Grandpa?

Farmer: I'm planting some potatoes. It's .... time of the year for that. (good)

Grandson: I think potatoes are .... vegetables... (mysterious)

Farmer: Why? To me they are .... thing to plant and .... food to eat. (easy / delicious)

Grandson: Because we don't see the potatoes growing. How do you know if they are good?

Farmer: Well, the .... is to believe in your experience. (important)

3 Complete the sentences with *who* or *which*.

a Mary is the girl .... is talking to the teacher.

b Sydney is the city .... is the capital of Australia.

c You don't like the comic books .... I read.

d The book .... I am reading is excellent.

e That is the librarian .... works in my school.

f I can't remember the name of the president .... was impeached.

g The sandwiches .... my mother prepares are much better.

4 Choose the correct alternative.

a I'm going to eat .... eggs for lunch.
○ some ○ any

b It's very quiet here. Let's play .... music.
○ some ○ any

c We don't have .... rooms available now.
○ some ○ any

d If you have .... time, I'd like to talk to you.
○ some ○ any

e Is there .... money in your pocket?
○ some ○ any

f Would you like .... coffee?
○ some ○ any

g We have a test tomorrow, so we don't have .... time to play video games.
○ some ○ any

Review 139

Grammar Reference

Unit 1

Verb *to be* vs. other verbs

1 Compare:

Affirmative (you / we / they)

to be	You	are	Brazilian.
other verbs	You	live	in Brazil.

Affirmative (he / she / it)

to be	She	is	American.
other verbs	She	lives	in the USA.

Negative

to be	You	aren't	Brazilian.
other verbs	You	don't live	in Brazil.

Negative

to be	She	isn't	American.
other verbs	She	doesn't live	in the USA.

Interrogative

to be	Are	you	–	Brazilian?
other verbs	Do	you	live	in Brazil?

Interrogative

to be	Is	she	–	American?
other verbs	Does	she	live	in the USA?

2 Write sentences with the words given and the appropriate form of the verbs.

a He / teacher (to be, negative)

....

b They / horror movies (to like, interrogative)

....

c Mary / Spanish (to study, interrogative)

....

d You / tall (to be, affirmative)

....

e He / in an apartment (to live, affirmative)

....

f We / soccer (to like, negative)

....

g Saturday / your favorite day of the week (to be, interrogative)

....

h I / always / breakfast at home (to have, affirmative)

....

i Mario / brothers or sisters (to have, negative)

....

Unit 2

Comparative

1 Read.

	Adjectives	Rules	Comparatives	Special spelling rules
short (adjectives with one syllable or two syllables ending in -y)	long tall big easy small cute	adjective + -er than	longer than taller than bigger than easier than smaller than cuter than	For adjectives ending in consonant, vowel, consonant (like **big**), we double the last consonant + **-er** to form the comparative. For adjectives ending in **-y** (like **easy**), we remove the **-y** and include **-ier** to form the comparative. For adjectives ending in **-e** (like **cute**), we only include **-r** to form the comparative.
long (adjectives with two or more syllables)	difficult interesting boring athletic beautiful intelligent modern wonderful	more (adjective) than	more difficult than more interesting than more boring than more athletic than more beautiful than more intelligent than more modern than more wonderful than	–
exceptions	good bad far	–	better than worse than farther than	–

2 Write sentences with the comparative form of the adjectives in parentheses.

a a little dog / a little cat (cute)

b Jim Carey / Adam Sandler (funny)

c Technology / Geology (interesting)

d your index finger / your middle finger (short)

e to be sick / to be sad (bad)

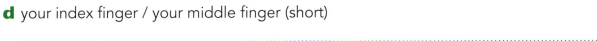

f birthdays / Christmases (good)

g singing / dancing (difficult)

Grammar Reference

Unit 3

Used to – affirmative

1 Study this example.

Subject	Used To	Verb	Complement
We	used to	live	in a house.

2 Write sentences about...

  a something you used to do when you were 10 years old.
  I used to stay with my grandmother when I was 10 years old.

  b something you used to watch on TV after school.
  ....

  c something you used to eat a lot of when you were younger.
  ....

  d something you used to do on the Internet.
  ....

  e something you used to wear.
  ....

3 Write sentences using **used to** and the words in parentheses.

  a (car – new)

  ....

  b (work – factory)

  ....

  c (walk – with my grandparents)

  ....

Grammar Reference

Unit 4

Verb *to be* – past

1 Study these examples.

Affirmative		
You We They	were	
		at home last nigth.
I He She It	was	

Negative			
You We They	were		
		not	at home last nigth.
I He She It	was		

Interrogative		
Were	you we they	
		at home last nigth?
Was	I he she it	

2 Complete this dialog with the past of the verb to be.

Man: Wait. I can't find my passport!

Woman: .... it in your bag?

Man: No, it .... in my pocket.

Woman: .... it there this morning?

Man: I don't think so. We .... at the zoo this morning and the passport .... at the hotel room.

Woman: But it .... on the table this morning.

Man: It ....? I .... sure I put it on the table yesterday.

Woman: We .... at the bank yesterday too. I think it is there.

Man: Maybe. Let's go there and check.

3 Write sentences using the verb to be in the past and the words given.

a They / at the party / last night (negative)

....

b Carol / at home / this morning (interrogative)

....

c I / sad / about my school grades (afffirmative)

....

d You / with Steven / at the game (interrogative)

....

Grammar Reference

Unit 5

There to be in the past

1 Study these examples.

There was a building here.

There weren't any families living in the building at the time of the demolition.

> there were/weren't + plural noun
> there was/wasn't + singular noun

2 Complete with **there to be** in the past (affirmative or negative).

In the past, ... cars on the streets so .... traffic. The city was very small and .... many people living in apartment buildings. .... pollution and people were healthier. But it was not perfect, ... problems too: the streets were dirty, ... organized crime, and .... telephones in every house.

3 Describe the changes in the decoration of the living room. Use the present or past of **there to be**.

Last year

Today

There were two black posters on the wall; now there aren't posters.

....
....
....
....
....

144   Grammar Reference

Unit 6

Superlative

1 **Study these examples.**

	Adjectives	Rules	Superlatives	Special spelling rules
short (adjectives with one syllable or two syllables ending in -y)	long tall big easy small cute	the adjective + **-est**	the longest the tallest the biggest the easiest the smallest the cutest	For adjectives ending in consonant, vowel, consonant, we double the last consonant + -est to form the superlative. For adjectives ending in **-y**, we remove the **-y** and include **-ier** to form the superlative. For adjectives ending in **-e**, we only include **-r** to form the superlative.
long (adjectives with two or more syllables)	difficult interesting boring athletic beautiful intelligent modern wonderful	the most (adjective)	the most difficult the most interesting the most boring the most athletic the most beautiful the most intelligent the most modern the most wonderful	–
exceptions	good bad far	–	the best the worst the farthest	–

2 **Write sentences with the superlative form of the adjectives in parentheses.**

a Lindsay / girl / in my class (cute)

....

b *Kung Fu Panda* / movie / last year (funny)

....

c Sciences / school subject / this year (interesting)

....

d Billy / student / P.E. class (short)

....

e C / grade / on my report card this semester (bad)

....

f This ballad / song on this album (good)

....

g Tango / dance style (difficult)

....

Grammar Reference

Unit 7

Relative pronouns – *who, which, that*

1 **Study these examples:**

> **Who** refers to people and **which** refers to things:
> I like the books **which** are on the table.
> I don't know the man **who** is talking to my father.

> **That** can be used for both people and things:
> I like the books **that** are on the table.
> I don't know the man **that** is talking to my father.

2 **Complete with who or which.**

  a A smartphone is a phone ………………… is used for communication and computing functions.

  b The people ………………… live on my street are very quiet.

  c A nurse is a person ………………… works in a hospital.

  d He is the only Japanese actor ………………… is famous internationally.

  e My cousin ………………… lives in New York is visiting me this week.

  f The girl ………………… studies English with me is very intelligent.

3 **Combine the two sentences. Use who or which.**

  a Lindsay / girl / in my class (cute)
  Celia is a scientist who studies viruses.

  b Aaron is a musician. Aaron likes jazz.
  ....

  c Green tea is a type of tea. Green tea brings health benefits.
  ....

  d Theodore is my uncle. He was born in Jamaica.
  ....

  e This bike has two wheels. The wheels are made of carbon.
  ....

  f Ostriches are a type of bird. Ostriches can't fly.
  ....

Grammar Reference

Unit 8

Countable / Uncountable nouns

1 **Study these tables.**

Countable	Uncountable
people, objects, names, animals, numbers, etc.	time, money, milk, air, juice, etc.

	Affirmative	Negative	Interrogative
Some	X		
Any		X	X

2 **Complete these sentences with some or any.**

a Daisy was at home with .... school friends.

b William doesn't have .... friends in school.

c Does she have .... brothers or sisters?

d It's 1 p.m. Let's eat .... food.

e I'm thinking about putting .... posters on the walls.

f There aren't .... text messages in my cell phone now.

g I don't want .... meat for dinner tonight!

h Unfortunately, I don't have .... good news for you.

i There isn't .... homework today! But I have to review .... lessons.

j Do you know .... famous artist?

3 **Check the correct option for the underlined words.**

a They add some <u>chemicals</u> in food in factories.

   ◯ countable   ◯ uncountable

b Do you have any <u>free time</u> tomorrow?

   ◯ countable   ◯ uncountable

c She doesn't have any <u>pets</u> at the moment.

   ◯ countable   ◯ uncountable

d I'm learning some <u>words</u> in German with my friend.

   ◯ countable   ◯ uncountable

e I think I'll have some <u>coffee</u> with my milk.

   ◯ countable   ◯ uncountable

f I need some <u>time</u> to think about it.

   ◯ countable   ◯ uncountable

Grammar Reference

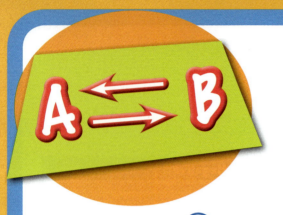

UNIT 2 Page 29

1 Listen and read. 🎧 7

A: <u>I have pimples all over my face</u>. What should I do?

B: You should <u>wash your face very well twice a day</u>.

B: You shouldn't <u>pop your pimples; they can get infected</u>.

A: OK, thanks for the advice.

2 Work with a partner.

a Student B: Student A is having some problems. Listen to them and choose the best advice to give him/her.

ADVICE

YES
- See a gynecologist to learn more about breast growth.
- Talking is always excellent therapy. Share your feelings with family, friends, or a trusted adult.
- Talk to your PE teacher. He/She can select physical activities to help you.
- Talk to your parents or a teacher about it. They can answer all your questions.

NO
- Do something just because everyone does it. Some people develop faster than others and this is normal.
- Let your bad mood hurt the people around you. If you feel you crossed a line, apologize.
- Stop physical exercises.
- Be afraid to ask questions. Information can save your life!

b Student B: You are having some problems. Talk to Student A and ask for advice.

PROBLEMS
- I have a lot of hair under my arms.
- My voice is cracking.
- I don't know how to use pads.
- I'm gaining too much weight.

UNIT 5 Page 86

1 Listen and read. 🎧 27

A: Look before you leap? I'm not sure I understand what you mean.

B: I mean you should check your possibilities before making a decision.

A: Oh, I get it now.

A: Hmm… I still don't get it. I'll look it up in a dictionary.

> **Other ways to ask for clarification**
> The meaning is not very clear to me.
> What are you trying to say?
> What does that mean?

2 Work with a partner.

a Student B: Student A will ask you to clarify the meaning of the proverbs below.

The grass is always greener on the other side: We look at other people's lives and possessions and think that they are better than ours but, in fact, they aren't.

No pain no gain: you have to make an effort to get what you want.

Birds of a feather flock together: people get together with people who have similar interests.

b Student B: Read the proverbs below and ask Student A to clarify them.

Too many cooks spoil the broth.

Better safe than sorry.

When in Rome, do as the Romans do.

A ⇄ B

149

UNIT 6 Page 95

1 Listen and read. 🎧 30

A: Justin Bieber is an autodidact. He learned to play the piano, drums, guitar, and the trumpet without help.
B: I can't believe it!

Other expressions
No kidding!
Are you for real?
Come on!
That blows my mind.

2 Work with a partner.

a Student B: Student A will read some facts to you. Listen to them and react.

b Student B: Now read the facts below to Student A.

Scott Flansburg can make complicated mathematical calculations faster than a calculator	Tutankhamun was the youngest king of ancient Egypt at the age of 9.
Junrey Balawing is the shortest man in the world, with 59.93 centimeters.	Usain Bolt can run 100 meters in 9.58 seconds.

A ⇌ B

Minidictionary

English-Portuguese

More than 800 entries!

WITH STAR RATING

adj. = adjective
adv. = adverb
conj. = conjunction
deter. = determiner
interj. = interjection
mod. v. = modal verb
n. = noun
numb. = number
prep. = preposition
pron. = pronoun
v. = verb

All red words have a "star rating":

★★★ The most common and basic English words

★★ Very common words

★ Fairly common words

A

a lot of /eɪ lat əv/ adv. muito (de) *There is a lot of water in the ocean.*

ability /ə'bɪləti/ noun ★★★ habilidade *He has the ability to roll his tongue.*

about /ə'baʊt/ adv. prep. ★★★ sobre *I like to talk about films.*

above /ə'bʌv/ adv. ★★★ acima *The roof is above the house.*

absent /'æbsənt/ adj. ★ ausente *Jackie is absent today because she is ill.*

accept /ək'sept/ v. ★★★ aceitar *They accept cash and cards in this shop.*

accident /'æksɪdənt/ n. ★★★ acidente *It was not on purpose; it was an accident.*

according to /ə'kɔrdɪŋ ,tu/ prep. ★★ de acordo com *According to the teacher, this exercise is easy.*

across /ə'krɔs/ adv. ★★★ do outro lado de *There is a hostel across the street.*

adjust /ə'dʒʌst/ v. ★★ ajustar, acertar *It took her two years to adjust to life in England.*

adopted /ə'daptəd/ adj. adotado *Are both of their kids adopted?*

advertise /'ædvər,taɪz/ v. ★★ anunciar *They advertise all kinds of products on TV.*

advice /əd'vaɪs/ noun ★★★ conselho *My friend Callie always gives me good advice.*

affect /ə'fekt/ v. ★★★ afetar *The disease affects many different organs of the body.*

after /'æftər/ adv. conj. prep. ★★★ depois *I brush my teeth after eating.*

after that /'æftər ðæt/ phrase depois disto *What's next after that?*

again /ə'gen/ adv. ★★★ novamente *I watched Twilight again yesterday.*

age /eɪdʒ/ n. ★★ idade, era *What's his age? He's eleven.*

aggressive /ə'gresɪv/ adj. ★★ agressivo *Today's executives are hungry, competitive, and aggressive.*

agree /ə'gri/ v. ★★★ concordar *We all agree that we should celebrate this event.*

all /ɔl/ adv. deter. prep. pron. ★★★ tudo, todos, *All my friends love sports.*

allergic /ə'lɜrdʒɪk/ adj. alérgico *I'm allergic to nuts.*

allergy /'ælərdʒi/ n. alergia *She has an allergy to cow's milk.*

almanac /'ɔlmə,næk/ n. almanaque *An almanac is a publication full of useful information.*

along /ə'lɔŋ/ adv. prep. ★★★ ao long de *Let's walk along the river.*

also /'ɔlsoʊ/ adv. ★★★ também *Luisa is my sister, but she is also my friend.*

although /ɔl'ðoʊ/ conj. ★★★ embora *Although it is raining, they want to swim.*

always /'ɔl,weɪz/ adv. ★★★ sempre *I always watch movies on the weekend.*

among /ə'mʌŋ/ prep. ★★★ entre muitos, dentre *There are two apples among the fruits in the basket.*

anniversary /,ænɪ'vɜrs(ə)ri/ n. ★★ aniversário de data *It's my grandparents' 50th anniversary.*

annoying /ə'nɔɪɪŋ/ adj. ★★ incômodo *What's really annoying is that we made the same mistake last time.*

another /ə'nʌðər/ pron. ★★★ outro *There's another news show at 10 o'clock.*

answer /'ænsər/ n. v. ★★★ resposta, responder *The correct answer is B.*

appearance /ə'pɪrəns/ n. ★★★ aparência *The twins are almost identical in appearance.*

appreciate /ə'priʃi,eɪt/ v. ★★ apreciar *She feels that her family doesn't really appreciate her.*

appropriate /ə'proʊpriət/ adj. ★★★ apropriado *Fill in the blank with the appropriate word.*

apt /æpt/ adj. ★ apto *He is apt to drive after two hours.*

arm /ɑrm/ n. ★★★ braço *I put my arm around his shoulders.*

arrive /ə'raɪv/ v. ★★★ chegar *The taxi will arrive at 8 o'clock.*

article /'ɑrtɪk(ə)l/ n. ★★★ artigo *In English, a and an are articles.*

artifact /'ɑrtɪ,fækt/ n. ★ artefato *You can see Indian artifacts and relics in this museum.*

artist /'ɑrtɪst/ n. ★★★ artista *Their lead singer has left to become a solo artist.*

asset /'æset/ n. ★★ bens *You're an asset to our team.*

assume /ə'sum/ v. ★★★ presumir *I think we can assume that he is out of town.*

astronomy /ə'stranəmi/ n. ★★★ astronomia *Astronomy is the study of the cosmos.*

at /æt/ prep. ★★★ em *We leave school at 1 o'clock.*

athlete /'æθ,lit/ n. ★ atleta *Severino has been an athlete since he was 5 years old.*

athletic /æθ'letɪk/ adj. ★ atlético *I want to learn how to be an athletic person.*

attention /ə'tenʃ(ə)n/ n. ★★★ atenção *May I please have your attention?*

attractive /ə'træktɪv/ adj. ★★★ atraente *We saw a less attractive side of his personality that day.*

audience /'ɔdiəns/ n. ★★★ público, audiência *The series has attracted an audience of more than 10 million.*

author /'ɔθər/ n. ★★★ autor *The author of the book is in town tonight.*

average /'æv(ə)rɪdʒ/ n. ★★★ média *Her performance on the test was below average.*

avoid /ə'vɔɪd/ v. ★★★ evitar *Vitor avoids eating meat.*

award /ə'wɔrd/ n. ★★★ prêmio *She won the Player of the Year award.*

awesome /'ɔsəm/ adj. incrível *2008 was an awesome year!*

B

bad /bæd/ adj. ★★★ mau *The teacher is in a bad mood today.*

balanced /'bælənst/ adj. ★ equilibrado *A balanced diet contains lots of fruit and green vegetables.*

ball /bɔl/ n. ★★★ bola *We'll be outside playing ball until dinner.*

be /bi/ v. ★★★ ser *The orchestra will be conducted by David Norton.*

152   **Minidictionary**

be able to /bi ˈeɪb(ə)l tə/ phrase ser capaz de *Mirian is able to take care of herself.*

be born phrasal verb nascer *He was born in November, 1964.*

because /bɪˈkɔz/ conj. ★★★ porque *The floor is wet because it rained.*

before /bɪˈfɔr/ adv. ★★★ antes *Brush your teeth before going to bed.*

befriend /bɪˈfrend/ v. tornar-se amigo *We befriended Jane and Sally many years ago.*

begin /bɪˈgɪn/ v. ★★★ começar *The ceremony is due to begin at noon.*

beginning /bɪˈgɪnɪŋ/ n. ★★★ começo *We missed the beginning of the film.*

behavior /bɪˈheɪvjər/ n. ★★★ comportamento *Anna was sick of her brother's annoying behavior.*

believe /bɪˈliv/ v. ★★★ acreditar *Astronomers knew the Earth was round, but few people believed it.*

below /bɪˈləʊ/ adv. ★★★ abaixo *The basement is below the house.*

belt /belt/ n. ★★ cinto *She is wearing a brown belt with a pink dress.*

besides /bɪˈsaɪdz/ adv. prep. ★★ além disso *A lot of them are studying other languages besides Italian.*

best /best/ adj. ★★★ melhor *Rory and Jade are best friends.*

better /ˈbetər/ adj. ★★★ melhor *Fernando is better in math than Cláudio.*

between /bɪˈtwin/ adv. ★★★ entre *The church is between the bank and the supermarket.*

bike /baɪk/ n. ★★ bicicleta *Their favorite sport is to ride a bike.*

birth rate n. taxa de natalidade *The birth rate is decreasing in Brazil.*

bitterness /ˈbɪtərnəs/ n. amargor *I don't like the bitterness of this fruit.*

black /blæk/ n. ★★★ preto *Jim has black hair.*

blackness /ˈblæknəs/ n. negritude *She disappeared into the blackness of the night.*

blessing /ˈblesɪŋ/ n. ★ bênção *It's a blessing that your children live so near.*

blond /bland/ adj. ★ loiro *He used to be blond, but now he has gray hair.*

blood pressure n. pressão arterial *When your blood pressure is low, have some salt.*

blue /blu/ n. ★★★ azul *The sky is blue.*

blurb /blɜrb/ n. resenha na contracapa *Read the blurb for a summary of the book.*

board game /bɔrd geɪm/ n. jogo de tabuleiro *Monopoly is Ray's favorite board game.*

body /ˈbadi/ n. ★★★ corpo **body tricks** truques com o corpo *My body hurts because I exercised too much.*

bone /boʊn/ n. ★★★ osso *She fell and broke a bone in her foot.*

book /bʊk/ n. ★★★ livro *This atlas is my least favorite book.*

bookmark /ˈbʊkˌmark/ n. marcador de página *The bookmark is on page 7.*

both /boʊθ/ det. pron. ★★★ ambos *Both my parents are doctors.*

bottom /ˈbatəm/ n. ★★★ embaixo *The Titanic is at the bottom of the ocean.*

box /baks/ n. ★★★ caixa *Put the toys into the box.*

boxing /ˈbaksɪŋ/ n. boxe *Boxing is becoming a popular sport.*

boy /bɔɪ/ n. ★★★ menino *Mr. and Mrs. Wylie have three boys and a girl.*

bra /bra/ n. ★ sutiã *This bra is too small for me.*

brand /brænd/ n. ★★ marca, logomarca *Lucas does not care about brands.*

break /breɪk/ v. ★★★ quebrar *Break the spaghetti in half and put it into the boiling water.*

breast /brest/ n. ★★ seio *She had small round breasts.*

bride /braɪd/ n. ★ noiva *The bride was not wearing white, but blue.*

bridge /brɪdʒ/ n. ★★★ ponte *We walked across a wooden bridge.*

bring /brɪŋ/ v. ★★★ trazer *You cannot bring pets to school.*

broadband /ˈbrɔdˌbænd/ n. banda larga *The computers in our school have broadband internet connection.*

brother /ˈbrʌðər/ n. ★★★ irmão *My brother is eight years old.*

brown /braʊn/ adj. ★★★ marrom *Lee's hair is brown.*

brush /brʌʃ/ v. n. ★★ escovar; escova **hair brush** escova de cabelo *Brush your hair and change your clothes.*

build /bɪld/ v. ★★★ construir *They are building a shopping mall near my house.*

built-in /bɪltɪn/ adj. integrado *There is a built-in voice recorder in this camera.*

burly ˈbɜrli/ adj. homem forte e robusto *My granddad was a tall and burly man.*

but /bʌt/ conj. ★★★ mas *It is hot, but windy.*

button /ˈbʌt(ə)n/ n. ★★ botão *Just press this button to start the computer.*

buy /baɪ/ v. ★★★ comprar *I buy food for the week.*

by /baɪ/ prep. ★★★ por *Helen and Hayley go to the university by bus.*

by the way phrase aliás *By the way, he is in town tonight.*

C

cafeteria /ˌkæfəˈtɪriə/ n. cantina *The students meet in the cafeteria for lunch.*

cake /keɪk/ n. ★★★ bolo *Carrot cake is my favorite dessert.*

can /kæn/ v. n. ★★★ poder, lata *I have more than fifty cans of soda.*

cap /kæp/ n. ★★ boné *Wear a cap when inside the caverns.*

car /kar/ n. ★★★ carro *My aunt's car is red.*

cardboard /ˈkardˌbɔrd/ n. ★ cartolina *Glue your photos onto the cardboard.*

career /kəˈrɪr/ n. ★★★ carreira *Rosen had decided on an academic career.*

carry /ˈkeri/ v. ★★★ carregar *Can you carry these bags?*

cassette /kəˈset/ n. ★ fita cassete *This is a very old cassette.*

cat /kæt/ n. ★★★ gato *Felix is a black cat.*

catch /kætʃ/ v. ★★★ pegar *We catch the bus at that stop over there.*

cause /kɔz/ v. ★★★ causa *The rain caused many problems.*

celebrity /səˈlebrəti/ n. ★ celebridade *She is not a celebrity; she is a real artist.*

cello /ˈtʃeloʊ/ n. violoncelo *This quartet is composed by a violin, a flute, and two cellos.*

certain /ˈsɜrt(ə)n/ adj. certeza, certo *I am certain he is in school today.*

chairman /ˈtʃermən/ n. ★★★ presidente (empresa / instituição) *Ron is the chairman of that oil company.*

change /tʃeɪndʒ/ v. n. ★★★ trocar, troco *You can keep the change.*

charming /ˈtʃarmɪŋ/ adj. ★★ charmoso *There are lots of charming little restaurants along the river.*

cheap /tʃip/ adj. ★★★ barato *People should have access to cheap, fresh food.*

check /tʃek/ v. ★★★ checar, marcar *Check the correct answers.*

Minidictionary 153

cheerful /'tʃɪrf(ə)l/ adj. ★ alegre *Stephen was a cheerful, affectionate child.*

chief /tʃif/ n. ★★★ chefe *She is the editor in chief in our company.*

choice /tʃɔɪs/ n. ★★★ escolha *Our aim is to provide greater choice for consumers.*

choose /tʃuz/ v. ★★★ escolher *I always choose pineapple ice cream.* **choice** escolha

chubby /'tʃʌbi/ adj. gordinho *He is not fat, just chubby.*

city /'sɪti/ n. ★★ cidade *São Paulo is the biggest Brazilian city.*

clarification /ˌklɛrɪfɪ'keɪʃ(ə)n/ n. esclarecimento *We are seeking clarification from the judge.*

classmate /'klæsˌmeɪt/ n. colega de classe *Andrew is my classmate at school.*

clear /klɪr/ adj. claro *Are the instructions for the exercise clear?*

clearance /'klɪrəns/ n. permissão, liquidação *Foreign workers had to get clearance to enter the country.*

clearly /'klɪrli/ adv. ★★ claramente *Clearly we wouldn't want to upset anyone.*

close /kloʊz/ v. n. ★★★ fechar; próximo *It's windy; close the window, please.*

clothes /kloʊðz/ n. ★★★ roupas *Alice's clothes are new.*

clue /klu/ n. ★★ pista *The sentences have clues to discover the mystery.*

coach /koʊtʃ/ n. ★★ treinador *Our coach is also our PE teacher.*

coffee /'kafi/ n. ★★★ café *Helen drinks coffee with milk every morning.*

coherent /koʊ'hɪrənt/ adj. ★ coerente *This text is not coherent.*

coin /kɔɪn/ n. ★★ moeda *We have only three coins.*

color /'kʌlər/ v. n. ★★★ colorir, pintar; cor *The rainbow has seven colors.*

colorful /'kʌlərf(ə)l/ adj. ★ colorido *The skyline is quite colorful tonight.*

come /kʌm/ v. ★★★ vir *The stickers come with the album.*

come on phrasal verb vir *Come on, let's go!*

common /'kɒmən/ adj. ★★★ comum *Stuart is a common name in England.*

compete /kəm'pit/ v. ★★★ competir *They compete in three competitions a year.*

complain /kəm'pleɪn/ v. ★★★ reclamar *Those tourists complain all the time.*

complexion /kəm'plekʃ(ə)n/ n. ★ feição *She has a delicate complexion.*

compliment /'kɑmplɪmənt/ n. ★ cumprimento *He gave me a compliment for the composition.*

connect to phrasal verb relacionar-se com *He is connected to most of my friends.*

consequence /'kɑnsəkwəns/ n. ★★★ consequência *The positive result is a consequece of your correct actions.*

construction worker n. pedreiro *Andrew is a construction worker.*

consumption /kən'sʌmpʃ(ə)n/ n. ★★ consumação *Let´s control the light consumption at school.*

contact lenses n. lentes de contato *She wears contact lenses when she goes to parties.*

contain /kən'teɪn/ v. ★★★ conter *This bottle contains 500ml of water.*

container /kən'teɪnər/ n. ★★ contêiner *Please do not put empty containers in the fridge.*

contestant /kən'testənt/ n. ★★ competidor *The competition has four contestants this year.*

contribute /kən'trɪbjut/ v. ★★★ contribuir *We must contribute to the government with part of our income.*

cook /kʊk/ v. ★★★ cozinhar *Marnie will cook something delicious tonight.*

cool /kul/ adj. ★★★ legal *The Oasis concert was really cool.*

copy /'kɑpi/ n. ★★★ copiar *Please, copy the answers in your notebooks.*

cosmetics /kɑz'metɪks/ n. cosméticos *Barbra is crazy about cosmetics.*

country /'kʌntri/ n. ★★★ país *Brazil is the biggest country in Latin America.*

couple /'kʌp(ə)l/ n. ★★★ casal *There are twenty couples in that room.*

cowgirl /'kaʊˌgɜrl/ n. vaqueira *Nina has been a cowgirl since she was 4 years old.*

crash /kræʃ/ v. quebrar *My computer crashed yesterday.*

crowd /'kraʊd/ n. ★★★ multidão *There is a crowd of fans outside the stadium.* **crowded** lotado

culture /'kʌltʃər/ n. ★★★ cultura *Culture is as important as food and health.*

curious /'kjʊriəs/ adj. ★★ curioso *I am curious about the end of the story.*

curly /'kɜrli/ adj. ★ encaracolado *That funny dog has curly fur.*

customer /'kʌstəmər/ n. ★★★ cliente *This is a list of special customers.*

cut /kʌt/ v. ★★★ cortar *Cut this sheet of paper in three pieces.*

cut down phrasal verb podar *I will cut down some trees in our garden.*

cute /kjut/ adj. fofo *That little cat is so cute!*

D

daily /'deɪli/ adj. ★★★ diário *We exercise daily.*

daughter /'dɔtər/ n. ★★★ filha *Sally is Rory and Mary's daughter.*

day /deɪ/ n. ★★★ dia *I have a shower every day.*

dead /ded/ adj. ★★★ morto *There were two people injured and one dead victim in the accident.*

deal /dil/ v. ★★★ lidar *You should deal with that situation in a calmer way.*

dear /dɪr/ adj. ★★★ querido; querida *Dear John, I miss you.*

death /deθ/ n. ★★★ morte *Death is the end of life.*

decade /'dekeɪd/ n. ★★★ década *This is considered a dead decade for rock.*

decrease /dɪ'kris/ v. ★★ decrescer *Temperatures decrease in winter.*

delicious /dɪ'lɪʃəs/ adj. ★ delicioso *This carrot cake is delicious.*

demigod /'demiˌgad/ n. semideus *In mythology, heroes are considered demigods.*

demolition /ˌdemə'lɪʃ(ə)n/ n. demolição *This window was recycled from demolition.*

depose /dɪ'poʊz/ v. depor *The people deposed a corrupt president in that country.*

describe /dɪ'skraɪb/ v. ★★★ descrever *Look at the picture and describe what you see.* **description** descrição

develop /dɪ'veləp/ v. ★★★ desenvolver *Practice the techniques to develop your skills.*

dialog /'daɪəlɒg/ n. ★★ diálogo *Listen to the dialog between Bruno and Jeff.*

diet /'daɪət/ n. dieta *I can't eat chocolate. I am on a diet.*

dinner /'dɪnər/ n. ★★★ jantar *We have dinner at 8:00 p.m.*

direction /dɪ'rekʃ(ə)n/ n. ★★★ direção; sentido *Can you give me the directions to school?* **directly** diretamente

disagree /ˌdɪsə'gri/ v. ★★ discordar *We disagree on almost everything.*

154   **Minidictionary**

discipline /ˈdɪsəplɪn/ n. ★★★ disciplina *Discipline is a safe way to freedom.*

discus throw n. lançamento de disco *The discus throw is an Olympic sport.*

display /dɪˈspleɪ/ v. dispor; mostrar *Display the cards on the table.*

distance /ˈdɪstəns/ n. ★★★ distância *What's the distance between your home and school?*

distract /dɪˈstrækt/ v. ★ distrair *Distract the dog while I leave.*

diving /ˈdaɪvɪŋ/ n. mergulho *Diving is an extreme sport.*

do /du/ v. ★★★ fazer *Do your homework before watching TV.*

doctor /ˈdɑktər/ n. ★★★ doutor, médico *Callie's brother is a children's doctor, he is a pediatrician.*

doorkeeper /ˈdɔrˌkipər/ n. porteiro *The doorkeeper is not here today.*

doubt /daʊt/ n. ★★★ dúvida *I have no doubts about his sports abilities.*

down /daʊn/ adv. prep. baixo, para baixo *We watched the sun go down.*

draft /drɑːft/ n. ★★ rascunho *Before you write the text, make a draft to help you organize your ideas.*

draw /drɔ/ v. ★★★ desenhar *Draw your favorite fruit on a piece of paper.* **drawing**

drawing /ˈdrɔɪŋ/ n. ★★★ desenho *The drawing on the wall was a gift from my mother.*

dream /drim/ n. ★★ sonho *I never remember my dreams.*

dress /dres/ n. ★★★ vestido **doll dress** vestido de boneca *Lacey's dress is blue.*

dressmaker /ˈdresˌmeɪkər/ n. costureira *She went to a dressmaker to order her wedding dress.*

dull /dʌl/ adj. ★★ chato, sem graça *This is a dull game.*

during /ˈdjʊərɪŋ/ prep. ★★★ durante *The baby generally sleeps during the night.*

E

each /itʃ/ det. pron. ★★★ cada *Each apple costs 50 cents.*

earphones /ˈɪrˌfoʊns/ n. fones de ouvido *Use earphones to listen to the audio.*

easily /ˈizəli/ adv. ★★★ facilmente *I can solve this puzzle easily.*

easy /ˈizi/ adj. ★★★ fácil, facilmente *This exercise is really easy.* **easily** facilmente

easygoing /ˌiziˈgoʊɪŋ/ adj. fácil de conviver *He is an easygoing kid.*

edit /ˈedɪt/ v. ★★ editar *Edit and proofread your text before giving it to the teacher.*

egg /eg/ n. ★★★ ovo *Pamela loves fried eggs.*

embarrassed /ɪmˈberəst/ adj. ★ envergonhado *I felt embarrassed about my wet clothes.*

emperor /ˈempərər/ n. ★ imperador *Nero was a cruel Roman emperor.*

encourage /ɪnˈkʌrɪdʒ/ v. ★★★ encorajar *Encourage people to be nice to each other.*

energetic /ˌenərˈdʒetɪk/ adj. ★ energético *He is a smart and energetic boy.*

engage /ɪnˈgeɪdʒ/ v. ★★ prender a atenção *A good book always has a story that engages readers.*

engineer /ˌendʒɪˈnɪr/ n. ★★★ engenheiro *Mr. Carr is an electrical engineer.*

enjoy /ɪnˈdʒɔɪ/ v. ★★★ curtir, desfrutar *Nina enjoys playing with her dogs.*

entertain /ˌentərˈteɪn/ v. ★★ entreter *The children sang and danced to entertain the crowd.*

entry /ˈentri/ n. ★★★ entrada; postagem *They were charged with illegal entry into the U.S.*

eruption /ɪˈrʌpʃ(ə)n/ n. erupção *The eruption of the volcano closed the airport.*

ethnicity /eθˈnɪsəti/ n. etnicidade *Ethnicity is studied by social scientists.*

even /ˈiv(ə)n/ adv. ★★★ par *Two is an even number.*

everyday /ˈevriˌdeɪ/ adj. ★★★ todo dia *Most people now accept that computers are a part of everyday life.*

everyone /ˈevriˌwʌn/ pron. ★★★ todos *Everyone here is under 16 years old.*

everything /ˈevriˌθɪŋ/ pron. ★★★ tudo *I will do everything for this team.*

everywhere /ˈevriˌwer/ adv. conj. prep. ★★★ em todo lugar *Everywhere I look, I see flowers.*

exaggerated /ɪgˈzædʒəˌreɪtəd/ adj. exagerado *He is an exaggerated actor.*

exchange /ɪksˈtʃeɪndʒ/ v. ★★★ trocar *Let's exchange phone numbers.*

expedition /ˌekspəˈdɪʃ(ə)n/ n. ★★ expedição *We went on an expedition in the forest.*

expensive /ɪkˈspensɪv/ adj. ★★★ caro *This skirt is too expensive. I will buy the other one.*

explain /ɪkˈspleɪn/ v. ★★★ explicar *I will try to explain how this machine works.*

expulsion /ɪkˈspʌlʃ(ə)n/ n. expulsão *His expulsion from West Point was humiliating.*

extreme /ɪkˈstrim/ adj. ★★ extremo *Any negative temperature is considered extreme in Brazil.*

eye /aɪ/ n. ★★★ olho *Mandy has got blue eyes.*

F

fair /feə(r)/ adj. ★★★ feira *Bienal do Livro is a Brazilian book fair.*

family /ˈfæm(ə)li/ n. ★★★ família *There are in more than 60 members in my family.*

far /fɑr/ adj. ★★★ longe *Porto Velho is far from Curitiba.*

fast /fæst/ adj. ★★★ rápido *Deers run really fast.*

fat /fæt/ adj. ★★ gordo *Hippos are generally fat.*

favorite /ˈfeɪv(ə)rɪt/ adj. ★★ favorito *Stephen King is one of my favorite writers.*

feather /ˈfeðər/ n. ★ pena *This pillow is made of duck feathers.*

featherweight /ˈfeðərˌweɪt/ n. peso pena *Featherweight is a martial arts category.*

feature /ˈfitʃər/ n. ★★★ característica, especificidade *Each room has its own distinctive features.*

few /fju/ det. pron. ★★★ poucos *Students, you have just a few minutes to hand in your compositions.*

fighter /ˈfaɪtər/ n. ★★ lutador *Mike Tyson was a famous fighter.*

file /faɪl/ n. ★★★ arquivo *The insurance company may want to check your medical files.*

fill up phrasal verb encher *We need to fill up the car with gas before the trip.*

finally /ˈfaɪn(ə)li/ adv. ★★★ finalmente *We finally arrived home at midnight.*

find /faɪnd/ v. ★★★ encontrar **find out** descobrir *I need to find my keys.*

fine /faɪn/ adj. adv. n. ★★★ bem; multa *I feel fine.*

finger /ˈfɪŋgər/ n. ★★★ dedo *We use the index finger to point out something we want to show.* **fingernail** dedo da mão

finish /ˈfɪnɪʃ/ v. ★★★ terminar *I finish my homework before watching TV.*

Minidictionary

first /fɜrst/ numb. ★★★ primeiro
The first day of the week is Sunday.

fitness /ˈfɪtnəs/ n. em forma
She needs to improve her fitness.

flag /flæg/ n. ★★ bandeira
The Brazilian flag has four colors.

flat /flæt/ adj. ★★★ murcho; plano
*Your car's tire is flat. We must
change it.*

flattery /ˈflætəri/ n. elogia *She thinks
that a little flattery might get results.*

float /floʊt/ v. ★★ flutuar *A cloud
floated across the moon.*

fly /flaɪ/ v. ★★★ voar *Sometimes
it's cheaper to fly.*

follow /ˈfaloʊ/ v. ★★★ seguir
Follow good examples. **following**
seguinte

food /fud/ n. ★★★ comida *Food is
good for your body.*

foot /fʊt/ n. ★★★ pé *Mary slid her
feet into her sandals.*

force /fɔrs/ n. ★★★ força *May the
force be with you.*

forest /ˈfɔrəst/ n. ★★★ floresta
*Acid rain is already destroying large
areas of forest.*

forget /fərˈget/ v. ★★★ esquecer
*They never forget to call me on my
birthday.*

form /fɔrm/ v. n. ★★★ formar,
formulário, forma *Fill in the form
with information about you.*

fragility /frəˈdʒɪləti/ n. fragilidade
*The fragility of the economy causes
unemployment.*

friendly /ˈfren(d)li/ adj. ★★★
amigável *This dog has a friendly look.*

from /frəm/ prep. ★★★ de *Hiro is
from Japan.*

fun /fʌn/ n. ★★ diversão *Kids love
having fun.*

funny /ˈfʌni/ adj. ★★★ engraçado
I don't think that's funny.

fur /fɜr/ n. ★ pelo, pele (de animal)
She hates those fur coats.

furniture /ˈfɜrnɪtʃər/ n. ★★★
móveis *His house is all decorated
with antique furniture.*

G

gain /geɪn/ v. n. ★★★ obter; ganho
*The Green Party gains new members
every year.*

gather /ˈgæðər/ v. ★★★ reunir,
agrupar *Football fans gathered around
the TV in the corner of the bar.*

generate /ˈdʒenəˌreɪt/ v. ★★★
gerar *The new car factory will
generate a lot of jobs in the area.*

generation /ˌdʒenəˈreɪʃ(ə)n/ n.
★★★ geração *My mother was the
only one in her generation to go to
college.*

genetically /dʒəˈnetɪkli/ adv.
geneticamente *My height is
genetically enherited.*

get out phrasal verb sair *Get out of
my room.*

gift /gɪft/ n. ★★★ presente *He bought
generous gifts for all his family.*

girl /gɜrl/ n. ★★★ menina *Lucy is a
girl's name.*

give /gɪv/ v. ★★★ dar *Give me the
car keys.*

glad /glæd/ adj. ★★★ alegre
I'm glad to meet you.

glasses /ˈglasəz/ n. ★ óculos
My glasses are broken.

glue /glu/ v. ★ colar *You can glue
the pictures onto the card.*

go through phrasal verb passar por
He is going through a bad phase.

goddess /ˈgadəs/ n. deusa *Athena
is a Greek goddess.*

godfather /ˈgadˌfaðər/ n. padrinho
*Mick Jagger is the godfather of
rock-and-roll vocals.*

gold /goʊld/ n. ★★★ ouro *The
picture frames were made of solid gold.*

golden /ˈgoʊld(ə)n/ adj. ★★★
dourado *These rings are golden but
are not made of gold.*

good /gʊd/ interj. ★★★ bom
Ivan is a good friend.

gouache /gwaʃ/ n. tinta guache *He
did this piece of art with gouache.*

government /ˈgʌvərnmənt/ n.
★★★ governo *The government
must take measures.*

grandparent /ˈgræn(d)ˌperənt/ n.
★ avós; o avô ou a avó
Our grandparents are still alive.

grass /graːs/ n. ★★★ grama *Do
not step on the grass.*

gray /greɪ/ adj. ★★★ cinza *The
sky is really gray this afternoon.*

great /greɪt/ adj. ★★★ ótimo
Lucca is a great student.

greet /grit/ v. ★★★ cumprimentar
*Natalie rushed to open the door and
greet the guests.*

grow /groʊ/ v. ★★★ crescer *That
tree can grow to over 100 feet tall.*

growth /groʊθ/ n. ★★★
crescimento *The growth of technology
in this country is impressive.*

guarantee /ˌgerənˈti/ n. ★★
garantia *Massive investment is no
guarantee of success.*

guess /ges/ v. ★★★ adivinhar,
chutar *Guess who is here!*

guessing game n. jogo de adivinhação
Miming is a kind of guessing game.

guidelines /ˈgaɪdˌlaɪnz/ n. ★★★
regras *These are the guidelines for
the board game.*

H

habit /ˈhæbɪt/ n. ★★★ hábito,
costume *Drinking water is a healthy
habit.*

hair /her/ n. ★★★ cabelo *His hair
is red and short.*

haircut /ˈherˌkʌt/ n. ★ corte de
cabelo *I don't like his new haircut.*

hairdresser /ˈherˌdresər/ n.
★ cabeleireiro *Her father is a
hairdresser.*

hairstyle /ˈherˌstaɪl/ n. ★ estilo de
cabelo *Their hairstyle is really modern.*

half /hæf/ adj. adv. pron. ★★★
metade, meio **half price** *Would you
like the other half of my pizza?* **half
brother** meio-irmão **half sister**
meia-irmã

hammer throw n. lançamento de
martelo *The hammer throw is an
ancient game.*

handicapped /ˈhændiˌkæpt/ adj.
deficiente físico *This parking lot is
for handicapped drivers.*

handwriting /ˈhændˌraɪtɪŋ/ n. ★
letra cursiva *Molly's handwriting is
really beautiful; she studies calligraphy.*

hang /hæŋ/ v. ★★★ pendurar *Hang
your coat on the hanger inside the
wardrobe.*

happen /ˈhæpən/ v. ★★★
acontecer *The Bienal do Livro
happens every two years.*

happy /ˈhæpi/ adj. ★★★ feliz *I get
really happy when I go to the beach.*

hard /hard/ adj. ★★★ duro; difícil
*This sofa is not comfortable; it is too
hard.*

hat /hæt/ n. ★★★ chapéu *This is an
old hat.*

hate /heɪt/ v. ★★★ odiar
Garfield hates Mondays.

have /hæv/ v. ★★★ ter **have a
good day** tenha um bom dia
We have four tickets for the game.

head /hed/ n. ★★★ cabeça **heads
and tails** cara ou coroa *My head
hurts.* **headphone** fone de ouvido

headline /ˈhedˌlaɪn/ n. ★★
manchete *The headlines today are
about the elections.*

health /helθ/ n. ★★★ saúde *It is
important to take care of your health.*

healthy /ˈhelθi/ adj. ★★★ saudável
Eating salad is a healthy habit.

hear /hɪə(r)/ v. ★★★ ouvir *Can you hear that noise?*

heavy /ˈhevi/ adj. ★★★ pesado
Pasta is too heavy to eat at night.

heel /hil/ n. ★★ salto *These sandals have high heels.*

height /haɪt/ n. ★★★ altura
What's your height?

help /help/ v. n. ★★★ ajudar; ajuda
I need help with my homework.

hermetic /hərˈmetɪk/ adj. hermético
This package has an hermetic seal.

hero /ˈhɪroʊ/ n. ★★ herói *Elvis has been my hero since I was a little boy.*

high /haɪ/ adj. ★★★ alto *There are more than 50 floors in this building; it is very high.*

highway /ˈhaɪˌweɪ/ n. ★★ estrada
He was charged with obstructing the public highway.

hill /hɪl/ n. ★★★ morro *They climbed slowly to the top of the hill.*

hip /hɪp/ n. ★★ quadril *He fell downstairs and broke his hip.*

hold /hoʊld/ v. ★★★ segurar *Hold your breath and jump into the water.*

home /həʊm/ n. ★★★ lar, casa
What time are you coming home?
homeless sem teto

homemade adj. caseiro, feito em casa *Are the cakes homemade?*

homework /ˈhoʊmˌwɜrk/ n. lição de casa *We have two chapters to read for homework.*

hope /hoʊp/ v. n. ★★★ esperar; esperança *These young people have no hope for the future.*

horn /hɔrn/ n. ★★ buzina *A car honked its horn at me.*

horse /hɔː(r)s/ n. ★★★ cavalo *Riding horses is one of Paula's pastimes.*

housekeeper /ˈhaʊsˌkipər/ n. governanta *Housekeepers work a lot.*

hungry /ˈhʌŋgri/ adj. ★★ faminto
I'm so hungry; I need to eat something.

hunt /hʌnt/ v. ★★ caçar *Wild dogs usually hunt in groups.*

I

iceberg /ˈaɪsˌbɜrg/ n. iceberg *Titanic's accident was caused by an iceberg.*

idea /aɪˈdiə/ n. ★★★ ideia *What a brilliant idea!*

idol /ˈaɪd(ə)l/ n. ídolo *He had the chance to play against his idol.*

if /ɪf/ conj. ★★★ se *Call me if you need anything.*

illustrate ˈɪləˌstreɪt/ v. ★★★
ilustrar *Miriam used examples to illustrate her point.*

impersonal /ɪmˈpɜrs(ə)nəl/ adj. ★
impessoal *His manner was cold and impersonal.*

impolite /ˌɪmpəˈlaɪt/ adj. ★ mal educado *It would be impolite to leave the party so early.*

improve /ɪmˈpruv/ v. ★★★
melhorar *Our main objective is to improve educational standards.*

improvement /ɪmˈpruvmənt/ n.
★★★ melhoramento *The school is performing well, but we recognize the need for further improvement.*

increase /ɪnˈkris/ v. ★★★
aumentar *We have managed to increase the number of patients treated.*

index /ˈɪndeks/ n. ★★★ índice
Check the index to see the correct pages of the book.

inept /ɪˈnept/ adj. inapto *He is inept at riding horses.*

inequality /ˌɪnɪˈkwaləti/ n. ★
desigualdade *Wealth inequality is a problem in most countries.*

influence /ˈɪnfluəns/ n. ★★★
influência *The decision-making process will be free from outside influence.*

information /ˌɪnfərˈmeɪʃ(ə)n/ n.
★★★ informação **a piece of information** *This information is top secret.*

injured /ˈɪndʒərd/ adj. ★
machucado *The injured included three young children.*

inside /ˈɪnˌsaɪd/ adj. adv. pron.
★★★ dentro *There are eight fish inside this aquarium.*

inspiration /ˌɪnspɪˈreɪʃ(ə)n/ n. ★★
inspiração *Dreams are a rich source of inspiration for some writers.*

install /ɪnˈstɔl/ v. ★★ instalar *It's important to install an antivirus.*

intelligent /ɪnˈtelɪdʒənt/ adj. ★★
inteligente *Is there intelligent life elsewhere in the universe?*

interesting /ˈɪntrəstɪŋ/ adj. ★★★
interessante *This new movie is very interesting.* **interest** interesse

interview /ˈɪntərˌvju/ n. ★★★
entrevista *Justin Bieber's interview is at 4 o'clock.*

into /ˈɪntu/ prep. ★★★ em, no, na
He jumped into the river.

issue /ˈɪʃu/ n. ★★★ questão *It's a website devoted to environmental issues.*

J

jacket /ˈdʒækɪt/ n. ★★★ jaqueta
I want a jean jacket as a birthday present.

jar /dʒar/ n. ★ jarra *Put the jar of jam on the table, please.*

jeep /dʒip/ n. jipe *My car is a jeep.*

job /dʒɒb/ n. ★★★ trabalho
Heloisa leaves her job at 6 o'clock.

joke /dʒəʊk/ n. ★★ piada
Comedians make jokes easily.

just /dʒʌst/ adv. ★★★ só, apenas *He is not my brother, he is just a friend.*

justify /ˈdʒʌstɪˌfaɪ/ v. ★★ justificar
You'll be expected to justify your actions.

K

keep /kip/ v. ★★★ manter
Keep calm and carry on.

kill /kɪl/ v. ★★★ matar *The nurse will give you something to kill the pain.*

kind /kaɪnd/ adj. ★★★ gentil, tipo
The waiter was very kind to us.

king /kɪŋ/ n. ★★★ rei
Oswald became king in 634.

knee /ni/ n. ★★★ joelho *Bend your knees when you pick up heavy objects.*

know /nəʊ/ v. ★★★ saber *I know how to draw a castle.*

knowledge /ˈnɑlɪdʒ/ n. ★★★
conhecimento *We had no knowledge of the incident.*

L

label /ˈleɪb(ə)l/ n. ★★ etiqueta
Check the DVDs and their labels.

lake /leɪk/ n. ★★ lago *There were some boys swimming in the lake.*

language /ˈlæŋgwɪdʒ/ n. ★★★
língua *I can read body language.*

last /læst/ adj. adv. v. ★★★ último, durar *My sister is on the last train to Brighton.*

law /lɔ/ n. ★★★ lei *It is against the law to smoke here.*

lawyer /ˈlɔjər/ n. ★★★ advogado
Their cousin is a lawyer.

lazy /ˈleɪzi/ adj. ★★ preguiçoso *It was hot in the yard, but she was too lazy to move.*

lean /lin/ v. ★★★ apoiar-se *You can lean on the wall.*

learn /lɜː(r)n/ v. ★★★ aprender *We learn English at school.*

leather /ˈleðər/ n. ★★ couro *I don't wear leather shoes.*

left /left/ adj. ★★★ esquerda *Paul writes with his left hand.*

Minidictionary 157

leg /leg/ n. ★★★ perna *She sat down and crossed her legs.*

legend /'ledʒənd/ n. ★★ lenda *Here, according to legend, Robin Hood lies buried.*

length /leŋθ/ n. ★★★ comprimento *What's the length of this piece of wood?*

letter /'letər/ n. ★★★ carta **letter paper** papel de carta *Laurie sometimes receives letters.*

librarian /laɪ'brerɪən/ n. ★ bibliotecário *Her mother is a librarian.*

lid /lɪd/ n. ★★ tampa *Put the lid on the bottle.*

like /laɪk/ v. ★★★ gostar *Mirian really likes cats.*

listen to /'lɪs(ə)n/ v. ★★★ ouvir *Listen to your teacher.*

live /lɪv/ v. ★★★ viver *Our neighbors live next door.*

long /lɒŋ/ adj. ★★★ longo *She has very long hair.*

look /lʊk/ v. n. ★★★ olhar *Look at the sentence and find the mistake.*

look like phrasal verb parecer-se com *You and your brother really look like your father.*

lose /luːz/ v. ★★★ perder *They are training so hard because they cannot lose this game.*

loss /lɒs/ n. ★★★ perda *It was an ancient car anyway, so it was no great loss.*

love /lʌv/ n. v. ★★★ amor, amar *Dogs love playing.*

low /ləʊ/ adj. ★★★ baixo *The prices are really low in this store.*

luck /lʌk/ n. ★★ sorte *Good luck on your exams!*

lunch /lʌntʃ/ n. ★★★ almoço **lunch worker, -lady, -man** (cantineira, cantineiro) *The lunch worker prepares our snacks at school.*

M

machine /mə'ʃin/ n. ★★★ máquina *Use that machine to make coffee.*

magazine /'mægə,zin/ n. ★★★ revista *Seventeen is a magazine for teenagers.*

maintain /meɪn'teɪn/ v. ★★★ manter; sustentar *He works a lot because he has a big family to maintain.*

make /meɪk/ v. ★★★ fazer *Let's make a lemon cake for dessert.*

many /'meni/ adv. ★★★ muitos *There are many kinds of fish in the city aquarium.*

marathon /'merə,θan/ n. ★ maratona *The meeting turned out to be a marathon.*

marker /'mɑrkər/ n. ★ marcador; pincel atômico *Use the marker to write your answers onto the board.*

married /'mærid/ adj. ★★★ casado *Our geography teacher is married to our PE instructor.*

match /mætʃ/ v. n. ★★★ ligar, conectar; partida, palito de fósforo *Match the words to the pictures they represent.*

maze /meɪz/ n. labirinto *He is lost in the maze.*

mean /min/ v. ★★★ significar *What does "book" mean?*

meaning /'minɪŋ/ n. ★★★ significado *What's the meaning of this word?*

medication /,medɪ'keɪʃ(ə)n/ n. medicamento *He is on medication and should not consume alcohol.*

meet /mit/ v. ★★★ encontrar, conhecer *Sam meets his friends every Friday afternoon.*

mention /'menʃ(ə)n/ n. ★★★ mencionar; menção *He didn't mention her all evening.*

merge /mɜrdʒ/ v. ★★ mesclar *Two of Indonesia's top banks are planning to merge.*

metabolism /mə'tæbə,lɪzəm/ n. metabolismo *Exercise to speed up your metabolism.*

middle /'mɪd(ə)l/ n. adj. ★★★ meio *His middle name is Silva; his full name is Jae Silva Jones.*

mind /maɪnd/ n. mente *Our ideas are born in our minds.*

mirror /'mɪrər/ n. ★★★ espelho *Look at yourself in the mirror.*

missing /'mɪsɪŋ/ adj. ★★ faltante *There is a letter missing in this word.*

mix /mɪks/ v. n. misturar; mistura *Mix all the ingredients together.*

money /'mʌni/ n. ★★★ dinheiro *I need some money to buy popcorn.*

month /mʌnθ/ n. ★★★ mês *January is the first month of the year.*

mood swing phrase alterações de humor *Mood swings are common during puberty.*

moon /mun/ n. ★★ lua *How many moons does Jupiter have?*

more /mɔr/ adv. pron. ★★★ mais *I want more rice, please.*

morning /'mɔrnɪŋ/ n. ★★★ manhã *I wake up at 6:00 in the morning.*

mosaic /mou'zeɪɪk/ n. mosaico *The image is composed of little pieces that form a mosaic.*

mother /'mʌðər/ n. ★★★ mãe *My mother is a lawyer.*

motivation /,moutɪ'veɪʃ(ə)n/ n. ★★ motivação *Their real motivation is to make a profit.*

motorcycle /'moutər,saɪk(ə)l/ n. ★ motocicleta *He can't drive motorcycles, just cars.*

mountain /'maʊnt(ə)n/ n. ★★★ montanha *They went walking and climbing in the mountains.*

mouth /maʊθ/ n. ★★★ boca *You should cover your mouth when you sneeze.* **mouthwash** enxágue bucal

move /muv/ v. ★★★ mover, mudar-se *Our neighbors will move to another city.*

muscle /'mʌs(ə)l/ n. ★★★ músculo *These exercises are good for your stomach muscles.*

mysterious /mɪ'stɪrɪəs/ adj. ★★ misterioso *He died in mysterious circumstances.*

mythology /mɪ'θalədʒi/ n. mitologia *There are many gods and goddesses in mythology.*

N

name /neɪm/ n. ★★★ nome **last name** sobrenome *Sarandon is her last name.*

narrow /'nerou/ adj. ★★★ estreito *We are left with a relatively narrow range of options.*

nationality /,næʃə'næləti/ n. ★ nacionalidade *Your nationality tells where you come from.*

naturally /'nætʃ(ə)rəli/ adv. ★★ naturalmente *Testosterone is a hormone that occurs naturally in the human body.*

necessarily /,nesə'serəli/ adv. ★★★ necessariamente *Public spending necessarily affects the economy.*

need /nid/ v. ★★★ precisar *We need milk to make the ice cream.*

neighbor /'neɪbər/ n. ★★★ vizinho *Rosalyn is my neighbor and classmate.*

never /'nevər/ adv. ★★★ nunca *You should never cross when the light is red.*

nevertheless /,nevərðə'les/ adv. ★★ contudo *Nevertheless, the country has immense problems.*

new /njuː/ adj. ★★★ novo *These are my new sneakers.*

news /njuːz/ n. ★★★ notícias *I have good news for you.*

newspaper /'nuz,peɪpər/ n. ★★★ jornal, periódico *Celia reads the newspaper every morning.*

next /nekst/ adj. adv. det. pron. ★★★ próximo, próxima *I sit next to him.*

158   **Minidictionary**

nice /naɪs/ adj. ★★★ legal *He is a nice teacher.*

nickname /'nɪkˌneɪm/ n. ★ apelido *Joy is Joyce's nickname.*

nor /nɔr/ conj. ★★★ nem *James isn't a millionaire, nor is he rich.*

notepad /'noʊtˌpæd/ n. bloco de anotações *Use this notepad to write your ideas.*

now /naʊ/ adv. ★★★ agora *Now you can go home.*

nowadays /'naʊəˌdeɪz/ adv. ★★ hoje em dia *Most women work nowadays.*

nuisance /'nusəns/ n. ★ incomodação, chateação *The bugs in the software were a nuisance.*

nutritionist /nu'trɪʃ(ə)nɪst/ n. nutricionista *A nutritionist helps you with your eating habits.*

O

obesity /oʊ'bisəti/ n. ★ obesidade *Obesity is a problem for many American teenagers.*

object /'abdʒəkt/ n. ★★★ objeto *There are thousands of objects in the museum's collection.*

occur /ə'kɜr/ v. ★★★ ocorrer *The accident occurred at about 4:30a.m.*

ocean /'oʊʃ(ə)n/ n. ★★★ oceano *We live two blocks from the ocean.*

of /əv/ prep. ★★★ de *Blue is the color of the sky.*

offbeat /'ɔfˌbit/ adj. pouco usual *He is a little offbeat, but a nice person.*

offer /'ɔfər/ v. n. ★★★ oferecer, oferta **special offer** oferta especial, promoção *Today, the snack bar has a special offer on hamburgers.*

Olympic /ə'lɪmpɪk/ adj. olímpico *Volleyball is an Olympic sport.*

only /'oʊnli/ adv. ★★★ só, somente *This restroom is only for women.*

opening /'oʊp(ə)nɪŋ/ n. ★★★ abertura *The opening of the exhibition will be at 4 o'clock.*

order /'ɔ:(r)də(r)/ v. n. ★★★ pedir; pedido, ordem *Let's order some pizza for dinner.*

ostrich /'astrɪtʃ/ n. avestruz *An ostrich is also a bird!*

other /'ʌðə(r)/ adj. pron. ★★★ outro *I do not want this chair; I want the other one.*

outgrow /aʊt'groʊ/ v. crescer além da conta *In a few months, Felipe will outgrow all his clothes.*

outside /ˌaʊt'saɪd/ adj. adv. prep. ★★★ externo; do lado de fora; fora *They will build a factory outside town.*

own /əʊn/ adj. pron. ★★★ próprio *Dan has his own bedroom.*

oyster /'ɔɪstər/ n. ostra *You can find a pearl inside an oyster.*

P

package /'pækɪdʒ/ n. ★★★ pacote, embalagem *We offer a generous package including meals.*

pad /pæd/ n. ★ absorvente higiênico *Use pads during your period.*

pain /peɪn/ n. ★★★ dor *No pain, no gain.*

paint /peɪnt/ v. n. ★★★ pintar, tinta *Let's paint the fence.*

pants /pænts/ n. pl. ★★ calças *He is the one in the blue pants and gray shirt.*

parent /'perənt/ n. ★★★ pais; o pai ou a mãe *My parents are divorced.*

partner /'partnər/ n. ★★★ parceiro, colega, dupla *Ned and Alice are partners; they always work together.*

password /'pæsˌwɜrd/ n. ★ senha *I can't remember my email password.*

patient /'peɪʃ(ə)nt/ adj. n. ★★★ paciente *There are three patients waiting to talk to the doctor.*

pay /peɪ/ v. ★★★ pagar **pay attention** prestar atenção *Pay attention to the teacher's instructions.*

pencil /'pens(ə)l/ n. ★★ lápis *Can I write in pencil? No, only in pen.*

person /'pɜː(r)s(ə)n/ n. ★★★ pessoa (pessoas) **people** pessoas *Barack Obama is a famous person all over the world.*

perhaps /pər'hæps/ adv. ★★★ talvez *Perhaps you should study more before the test.*

period /'pɪriəd/ n. ★★★ ponto final, período; menstruação *Use a period at the end of a sentence.*

personality /ˌpɜrsə'næləti/ n. ★★★ personalidade *Certain personality traits may be inherited from our parents.*

phenomenon /fə'naməˌnan/ n. ★★ fenômeno *Violence in society is not a new phenomenon.*

philosopher /fɪ'lasəfər/ n. ★ filósofo *Plato was a famous Greek philosopher.*

physical /'fɪzɪk(ə)l/ adj. ★★★ físico *Physical exercise is good for your body and mind.*

picture /'pɪktʃər/ n. ★★★ ilustração, foto *Look at the pictures on page 56.*

pimple /'pɪmp(ə)l/ n. espinha *Some teens have pimples during their puberty.*

pin /pɪn/ n. ★★ malabar *Toss the pins up to juggle.*

place /pleɪs/ n. ★★★ lugar, local *I know where this place is; it's near my house.*

plagiarism /'pleɪdʒəˌrɪzəm/ n. plágio *Plagiarism is a crime among academics.*

platform shoes n. sandália anabela *Platform shoes make you look taller.*

player /'pleɪər/ n. ★★★ jogador; tocador *Ronaldo used to be a soccer player.*

pocket /'pakɪt/ n. ★★★ bolso *I have ten reais in my pocket.*

police officer n. ★ policial *My grandfather works as a police officer.*

politician /ˌpalə'tɪʃ(ə)n/ n. ★★★ político *Politicians are responsible for ruling the country.*

pop /pap/ v. ★★ espremer *You should not pop your pimples.*

portrait /'pɔrtrət/ n. ★★ retrato *This is a portrait of my whole family.*

post /poʊst/ v. n. ★ postar, postagem *I will post our photo on my blog.*

potato /pə'teɪtoʊ/ n. ★★ batata *Potatoes are very popular in Britain.*

power /'paʊər/ n. ★★★ poder *He has an amazing power of concentration.*

practice /'præktɪs/ v. n. ★★ praticar; prática *Let's practice this conversation in pairs.*

precocious /prɪ'koʊʃəs/ adj. precoce *He started singing at a precocious age.*

predispose /ˌpridɪs'poʊz/ v. predispor-se *Is there something that predisposes a nation to revolution?*

pregnant /'pregnənt/ adj. ★★ grávida *My sister is four months pregnant.*

prejudice /'predʒədɪs/ n. ★★ preconceito *We want to overcome prejudice against women in politics.*

presenter /prɪ'zentər/ n. apresentador *He is a TV presenter and actor.*

previously /'priviəsli/ adv. ★★★ previamente *She was previously employed as a research scientist.*

price /praɪs/ n. ★★★ preço *Students don't have to pay regular price; they have discount.*

pride /praɪd/ n. ★★ orgulho *She can certainly look back on her performance with pride.*

print /prɪnt/ v. n. ★★★ imprimir; impressão *Print six copies of this document.*

prize /praɪz/ n. ★★★ prêmio *The prize is a new computer.*

Minidictionary

probably /ˈprabəbli/ adv. ★★★ provavelmente *I'll cook a meal, probably lasagna or something.*

problem /ˈprabləm/ n. ★★★ problema *That still doesn't solve our problem.*

produce /prəˈdus/ v. ★★★ produzir *The body produces chemicals called endorphins to control pain.*

profession /prəˈfeʃ(ə)n/ n. ★★★ profissão *People in my profession have a duty to the public.*

prodigy /ˈpradədʒi/ n. prodígio *He was already considered a prodigy by the age of 7.*

prominence /ˈpramɪnəns/ n. proeminência *This case gave new prominence to the problem of domestic violence.*

pronounce /prəˈnaʊns/ v. ★★ pronunciar *I find some Japanese words very difficult to pronounce.*

proofread /ˈprufˌrid/ v. revisar (textos) *You should proofread your compositions before handing them in.*

protect /prəˈtekt/ v. ★★★ proteger *Wear a helmet to protect your head.* **protection** proteção **protective** protetor

proud /praʊd/ adj. ★★ orgulhoso *Our group is proud of our work.*

proverb /ˈpraˌvɜrb/ n. provérbio *Proverbs are popular sayings that are wise.*

provide /prəˈvaɪd/ v. ★★★ prover *This meal provides all the energy you need for the exercise.*

puberty /ˈpjubərti/ n. puberdade *Puberty is a period of great changes.*

publish /ˈpʌblɪʃ/ v. ★★★ publicar *They publish story books.*

purchase /ˈpɜrtʃəs/ v. n. ★★ comprar; compra *I need help to purchase something from the Internet.*

purse /pɜrs/ n. ★★ carteira feminina *Put the change in your purse.*

Q

question /ˈkwestʃ(ə)n/ n. ★★★ questão, pergunta **question mark** ponto de interrogação *I know the answer to this question.*

questionnaire /ˌkwestʃəˈner/ n. ★★ questionário *Complete the questionnaire with your own information.*

quiet /ˈkwaɪət/ adj. ★★★ quieto *I like this neighborhood because it is quiet and calm.*

R

rather /ˈræðər/ adv. ★★★ bem *He is rather intelligent for his age.*

read /rid/ v. ★★★ ler *Read the question and answer it in your notebook.*

reader /ˈridər/ n. ★★★ leitor *Wilma is a compulsive reader.*

reading /ˈridɪŋ/ n. ★★★ leitura *Reading is a great pastime.*

ready /ˈredi/ adj. ★★★ pronto *I am ready for the holidays.*

reality /riˈæləti/ n. ★★★ realidade *Francis does not like reality shows.*

recipe /ˈresəpi/ n. ★★ receita (culinária) *I know an easy apple pie recipe.*

recognize /ˈrekəgˌnaɪz/ v. ★★★ reconhecer *I hardly recognized you with a beard!*

recommendation /ˌrekəmenˈdeɪʃ(ə)n/ n. ★★ recomendação *Do you have any special recommendation?*

red /red/ adj. ★★★ vermelho *You must stop when the light is red.*

regret /rɪˈgret/ v. n. ★★ arrepender-se, arrependimento *No regrets, just good memories.*

reissue /ˌriˈɪʃu/ v. ★★★ relançar *They will reissue the first edition of the comics.*

release /rɪˈlis/ v. ★★★ lançar *The authorities recently released two political prisoners.*

reliable /rɪˈlaɪəb(ə)l/ adj. ★★ confiável *Maria is a reliable friend.*

remember /rɪˈmembər/ v. ★★★ lembrar *Remember to call me when you get there.*

repair /rɪˈper/ v. ★★ reparar, consertar *He had two operations to repair his left knee.*

reply /rɪˈplaɪ/ v. ★★★ responder *I hope they reply to my email.*

reputation /ˌrepjəˈteɪʃ(ə)n/ n. ★★★ reputação *He did not have a good reputation in his hometown.*

require /rɪˈkwaɪr/ v. ★★★ requerer, pedir *Working with children requires a great deal of patience.*

resistance /rɪˈzɪstəns/ n. ★★★ resistência *Vitamin C helps build resistance to infection.*

respected /rɪˈspektəd/ adj. ★ respeitado *Jerkis is a respected professor at the university.*

responsibility /rɪˌspansəˈbɪləti/ n. ★★★ responsabilidade *Doing the homework is the responsibility of the student.* **responsible** responsável

return /rɪˈtɜrn/ v. ★★★ retornar, voltar *When you finish the book, please return it to the library.*

ribbon /ˈrɪbən/ n. ★ fita *Jurema uses ribbons to tie back hair.*

rich /rɪtʃ/ adj. ★★★ rico *His invention has made him a rich man.*

ride /raɪd/ v. n. ★★★ dirigir, conduzir; corrida *Ana and Harry ride their bikes in the park every day.*

right /raɪt/ adv. ★★★ certo, direito *Our teacher is the one on the right of the photo.*

ring /rɪŋ/ n. ★★★ anel *Candy has a collection of rings.*

rise /raɪz/ v. n. ★★★ subir, ascenção *Temperatures rise in the summer.*

river /ˈrɪvər/ n. ★★★ rio *In São Paulo, there is a river called the Tietê.*

rodeo /roʊˈdeɪoʊ/ n. rodeio *Rodeos are common festivals in countryside towns.*

round /raʊnd/ n. ★★★ rodada *Come on, the boxing match is already in the second round.*

routine /ˌruˈtin/ n. ★★ rotina *We have a strict routine at school.*

rude /rud/ adj. ★★ rude *I don't want to seem rude, but I'd rather be alone.*

rule /rul/ n. ★★★ regra *Pay attention to the rules of the game.*

run /rʌn/ v. ★★★ correr *Our friends run 10 kilometers a day.*

runner /ˈrʌnər/ n. ★★ corredor *He is a professional runner.*

S

safe /seɪf/ adj. ★★★ seguro *It is safe to use banks through the Internet.* **safety** segurança

salutation /ˌsæljəˈteɪʃ(ə)n/ n. cumprimento *Hi is an informal salutation.*

same /seɪm/ adj. adv. pron. ★★★ mesmo *We have the same name: we are both called Raj.*

sandal /ˈsænd(ə)l/ n. sandália *Mercury used to wear golden sandals.*

sandwich /ˈsæn(d)wɪtʃ/ n. ★★ sanduíche *Irvin has ham and cheese sandwiches as a snack.*

say /seɪ/ v. ★★★ dizer *Say a number between one and ten.*

scar /skar/ n. ★ cicatriz *Priscila has two scars on her left arm.*

scared /skerd/ adj. ★★★ assustado *Joana is scared of scorpions.*

scarf /skarf/ n. ★ echarpe *She has a beautiful pink and purple scarf.*

school /skul/ n. ★★★ escola **school grade** ano escolar **school office** secretaria da escola *Where is your school?*

scissors /'sɪzərz/ n. pl. ★ tesoura *Cut this piece of paper with scissors.*

score /skɔr/ v. n. ★★★ marcar um ponto, resultado *The final score was 2 X 0.*

scrapbook /'skræp,bʊk/ n. álbum *My scrapbook is decorated with photos and messages from friends.*

seal /sil/ n. v. ★★ selo; selar *Seal the box with tape.*

seat /sit/ n. v. ★★ assento, sentar *Go back to yor seats and do the activity.*

second /'sekənd/ numb. ★★★ segundo *Second prize is a bicycle.*

see /si/ v. ★★★ ver *I love to see the sun rising.*

selfish /'selfɪʃ/ adj. ★ egoísta *Selfish people generally do not have many friends.*

send /send/ v. ★★★ enviar *Send your photo by email.*

sensitive /'sensətɪv/ adj. ★★★ sensível *Rogério is a very sensitive person.*

serious /'sɪriəs/ adj. ★★★ sério *It's not a serious problem – we should be able to fix it easily.*

shape /ʃeɪp/ n. v. ★★★ forma; formatar *This box has a square shape.*

share /ʃer/ v. ★★★ dividir, compartilhar *Let's share this piece of cake.*

shave /ʃeɪv/ v. ★ barbear, depilar *I cut myself while I was shaving.*

sheep /ʃip/ n. ★★ ovelha *Count sheep until you fall asleep.*

sheet /ʃit/ n. ★★★ lençol; folha de papel *The bed sheet is clean.*

shell /ʃel/ n. ★★ concha *I like picking up shells on the beach.*

shield /ʃiːld/ n. ★★ escudo *Use the shield to protect yourself.*

shirt /ʃɜrt/ n. ★★★ camisa **soccer shirt** camisa de futebol *I have a soccer shirt collection.*

short /ʃɔrt/ adj. ★★★ curto *Henry's hair is short.*

shorts /ʃɔrts/ n. pl. ★ shorts *We wear shorts during our PE classes.*

shot put n. arremesso de peso *My brother practices shot put.*

should /ʃʊd/ modal ★★★ deveria *We all should study before the exam.*

shoulder /'ʃoʊldər/ n. ★★★ ombro *She injured her shoulder in the accident.*

show /ʃoʊ/ v. ★★★ mostrar, apresentar *Show me your cards.*

show up phrasal verb aparecer *They always show up at the end of the parties.*

shy /ʃaɪ/ adj. ★ tímido *He is so shy he blushes when he talks.*

silly /'sɪli/ adj. ★★ bobo *Don't get upset over silly things that people say.*

simple /'sɪmp(ə)l/ adj. ★★★ simples *The answer is so simple.*

since /sɪns/ adv. conj. prep. ★★★ desde *We are friends since school.*

singer /'sɪŋər/ n. ★★ cantor *He is a popular Brazilian singer.*

single /'sɪŋ(ə)l/ adj. ★★★ solteiro *Debra's father is a single parent.*

sister /'sɪstər/ n. ★★★ irmã *Belle is Becky's sister.*

situation /ˌsɪtʃu'eɪʃ(ə)n/ n. ★★★ situação *The country is facing a very difficult economic situation.*

size /saɪz/ n. ★★★ tamanho *My T-shirt size is extra large.*

skeleton /'skelɪt(ə)n/ n. ★ esqueleto *The human skeleton is composed of more than a hundred bones.*

skill /skɪl/ n. ★★★ habilidade *Reading is my most developed skill in English.*

skinny /'skɪni/ adj. magrinho *She is such a skinny girl.*

skirt /skɜrt/ n. ★★ saia *I love wearing skirts during the summer.*

skull /skʌl/ n. ★★ caveira *My favorite T-shirt has skull on it.*

sleepy /'slipi/ adj. ★ sonolento *I am always sleepy in the morning.*

slim /slɪm/ adj. ★★ esbelto *This ballet dancer is so slim.*

slow /sloʊ/ adj. ★★★ vagaroso *A slow smile spread across her face.*

small /smɔl/ adj. ★★★ pequeno *I have a small doll called Poppy.*

smile /smaɪl/ v. n. ★★★ sorrir; sorriso *Smile and people will smile back at you.*

sneaker /'snikər/ n. tênis *Your brother's sneakers are stinky.*

snow /snoʊ/ n. ★★★ neve *This is the first time I see snow: it is beautiful.*

so /soʊ/ adv. conj. ★★★ tão *He is so smart! I'm impressed.*

soccer /'sakər/ n. ★ futebol *Soccer is a popular sport in Brazil.*

sock /sak/ n. ★ meia *There is a hole in your sock.*

soft /sɔft/ adj. ★★★ macio *My pillow is really soft and fluffy.*

soldier /'soʊldʒər/ n. ★★★ soldado *Soldiers work for the army.*

some /sʌm/ adv. det. pron. ★★★ algum *We need some sugar for the cake.*

someday /'sʌm,deɪ/ adv. algum dia *Someday we can go to the club together.*

something /'sʌmθɪŋ/ pron. ★★★ algo *I want something to eat.*

sound /saʊnd/ n. ★★★ som **sound effect** efeito sonoro *The sound of rain calms her down.*

source /sɔrs/ n. ★★★ fonte *Sugar is a great source of energy.*

speaker /'spikər/ n. ★★★ auto-falante *My stereo has two potent speakers.*

speech /spitʃ/ n. ★★★ fala, discurso *The queen made a wonderful speech.*

spoken /'spoʊkən/ adj. ★ falado *Spoken agreements are sometimes difficult to enforce.*

sponsor /'spansər/ n. ★ patrocinador *The cheese factory is the sponsor of our team.*

sport /spɔrt/ n. ★★★ esporte *Ron loves playing sports.*

sprint /sprɪnt/ n. ★ tiro (de corrida) *They will run 10 sprints this afternoon.*

square /skwer/ n. ★★★ quadrado *The garden has flower beds that form a perfect square.*

stability /stə'bɪləti/ n. ★★ estabilidade *The rise of nationalism could threaten the stability of Europe.*

stadium /'steɪdiəm/ n. ★ estádio *The match will take place at the municipal stadium.*

start /start/ v. ★★★ começar *The game starts at 5 o'clock.*

station /'steɪʃ(ə)n/ n. ★★★ estação *The bus station is in the city center.*

step /step/ n. ★★★ passo, degrau *There are 200 steps in this stair case.*

stimulate /'stɪmjə,leɪt/ v. ★★ estimular *These video games stimulate our brains.*

stone /stoʊn/ n. ★★★ pedra *The house is made of stone.*

store /stɔr/ n. ★★★ loja *We can buy the tickets for the game at the sports store.*

story /'stɔri/ n. ★★★ história *Ivy likes reading stories.*

storyteller /'stɔri,telər/ n. contador de história *Our teacher is also a storyteller; we love her stories.*

straight /streɪt/ adj. ★★ liso *Cris has long straight hair.*

strength /streŋθ/ n. ★★★ força *I didn't have the strength to get out of bed.*

strong /strɔŋ/ adj. ★★★ forte *Are you strong enough to carry that heavy box?*

Minidictionary   161

stubborn /'stʌbərn/ adj. ★ teimoso *Defenders of the city put up a stubborn resistance.*

student /'stud(ə)nt/ n. ★★★ estudante *There are 40 students in my class.*

subway /'sʌb,weɪ/ n. ★★ metrô *Do you take the bus or the subway to go to school?*

successful /sək'sesfəl/ adj. ★★★ bem sucedido *You have to study and work hard to be a successful person.*

such /sʌtʃ/ det. pron. ★★★ tal *He is such a nice friend!*

sugar /'ʃʊgər/ n. ★★★ açúcar *Harry likes his coffee with sugar.*

suitable /'sutəb(ə)l/ adj. ★ adequado *My dress is not suitable for the occasion.*

summary /'sʌməri/ n. ★★ sumário *See the summary to check if you understood the text.*

sunglasses /'sʌn,glæsəz/ n. óculos de sol *I always wear sunglasses at the beach.*

superhighway /,supər'haɪ,weɪ/ n. autoestrada *Information superhighway is a way to refer to the Internet.*

supply /sə'plaɪ/ v. ★★★ suprir *Can you supply a list of the guests?*

support /sə'pɔrt/ v. ★★★ apoiar *This institution supports handicapped children.*

sure /ʃʊr/ adj. ★★★ claro, certo *I am sure he is in the school.*

surprising /sər'praɪzɪŋ/ adj. ★★★ surpreendente *This is really susrping news.*

suspension /sə'spenʃ(ə)n/ n. ★★ suspensão *They got a suspension for talking during the test.*

sweetness /'switnəs/ n. douçura *One minute she's incredibly rude to me and the next she's all sweetness.*

sword /sɔrd/ n. ★★ espada *Knights used to fight with swords.*

T

table /'teɪb(ə)l/ n. ★★★ mesa *The book is on the table.*

take /teɪk/ v. ★★★ tomar, tirar, levar **take care** cuidar **take a photo** tirar uma foto *Take care of the plants while I'm traveling.*

talented /'tæləntəd/ adj. ★ talentoso *Mozart was a talented musician from childhood.*

talk /tɔk/ v. ★★★ falar *Talk to a classmate about your favorite hobbies.*

talk about phrasal verb falar sobre *Let's talk about our plans for the future.*

tall /tɔl/ adj. ★★★ alto *You must be tall to be a fashion model.*

tank top n. camiseta regata *Those athletes wear tank tops during the competitions.*

teacher /'titʃər/ n. ★★★ professor *Our teacher lives near the school.*

technology /tek'nɑlədʒi/ n. ★★★ tecnologia *Technology is in our daily lives all the time.*

teenager /'tin,eɪdʒər/ n. ★★ adolescente *Lee is fourteen; he is a teenager.*

temple /'temp(ə)l/ n. ★★ templo *A library is a temple of knowledge.*

temporary /'tempə,reri/ adj. ★★★ temporário *My aunt needs a temporary secretary.*

testes n. pl. testículos *Men generally have two testes.*

testimonial /,testə'moʊniəl/ n. testemunho *My friends write testimonials on my social network page.*

text /tekst/ n. ★★★ texto *Read the text and answer the questions.*
texting mensagem de texto

than /ðæn/ conj. prep. ★★★ do que (comparativo) *He is taller than me.*

thank /θæŋk/ v. ★★★ agradecer *Thank your mother for the cake.*

then /ðen/ adj. adv. ★★★ então, em seguida *I brush my teeth, and then I go to bed.*

thesaurus /θə'sɔrəs/ n. um livro que contém palavras com significados parecidos *Check this thesaurus for synonyms.*

these /ðiz/ adv. det. pron. ★★★ estes, estas *These are my cats, Mingau and Garfield.*

thin /θɪn/ adj. ★★★ magro *Mr. Burn is tall and thin.*

think /θɪŋk/ v. ★★★ pensar *It is good to think before speaking.*

though /ðoʊ/ adv. conj. ★★★ embora *He still argues, though he knows he's wrong.*

thousand /'θaʊz(ə)nd/ numb. ★★ mil *There are more than a thousand students in my school.*

throw /θroʊ/ v. ★★★ lançar, jogar *Throw the ball into the basket and score a point.*

ticket /'tɪkɪt/ n. ★★★ entrada, convite, bilhete **movie ticket** ingresso para o cinema *I have two tickets for the play.*

tie /taɪ/ n. v. ★★★ gravata; atar, prender *He has to wear a tie to work.*

time /taɪm/ n. ★★★ tempo *We have time for a coffee.*

tip /tɪp/ n. ★★★ dica *Can you give me some tips about the city?*

tire /'taɪr/ n. ★★ pneu *Our car has a flat tire.*

tiring /'taɪrɪŋ/ adj. cansativo *Doing these exercises is really tiring.*

tissue /'tɪʃu/ n. ★★ lenço *Use a tissue when you sneeze.*

title /'taɪt(ə)l/ n. ★★★ título *Write a title for your composition.*

together /tə'geðər/ adv. ★★★ junto *We go to our English classes together.*

token /'toʊkən/ n. token *I have five book tokens.*

tomorrow /tə'mɔroʊ/ adv. ★★★ amanhã *Today is Thursday; tomorrow is Friday.*

too /tu/ adv. ★★★ também (usado no fim da frase) *You love me and I love you too.*

top /tɑp/ n. ★★★ cima, em cima *The penguin is on the top of the fridge.*

toss /tɔs/ v. ★★ jogar, lançar *Let's toss the dice to see who's the winner.*

touch /tʌtʃ/ v.n. ★★★ tocar; toque *Stretch your arms and try to touch your toes.*

traffic /'træfɪk/ n. ★★★ trânsito *The traffic is terrible today; there are so many cars!*

train /treɪn/ n. ★★★ trem *This train leaves at midnight.*

training /'treɪnɪŋ/ n. ★★★ treinamento *We attend intensive training before the day of the competition.*

treatment /'tritmənt/ n. ★★★ tratamento *Resting is part of the treatment for your flu.*

trend /trend/ n. ★★★ tendência *Learning German is a new trend among teens.*

triathlon /traɪ'æθlən/ n. triátlon *A thriathlon is an activity composed of running, cycling, and swimming.*

trip /trɪp/ n. ★★★ viagem *This trip will take about seven hours.*

trousers /'traʊzərz/ n. pl. calças *These are my favorite trousers.*

true /tru/ adj. ★★★ verdadeiro *This is a true story.*

try /traɪ/ v. ★★★ tentar *They will try to learn Chinese!*

T-shirt n. ★ camiseta *Sandra has three white T-shirts.*

tunnel /'tʌn(ə)l/ n. ★★ túnel *To get to the beach we pass through five tunnels.*

turntable /'tɜrn,teɪb(ə)l/ n. vitrola *The DJs play on turntables in that club.*

twice /twaɪs/ adv. ★★★ duas vezes *I have swimming classes twice a week.*

type /taɪp/ v. n. ★★★ digitar; tipo *What is your favorite type of food?*

U

ugly /ˈʌgli/ adj. ★★ feio *Ugly is the opposite of beautiful.*

uncomfortable /ʌnˈkʌmfərtəb(ə)l/ adj. ★★ desconfortável *This bra is really uncomfortable.*

uncoordinated /ʌnkoʊˈɔrdɪˌneɪtəd/ adj. descoordenado *She's too uncoordinated to be a dancer.*

under /ˈʌndər/ adv. prep. ★★★ sob *There is a ball under my bed.*

underline /ˌʌndərˈlaɪn/ v. ★★ sublinhar *Underline the answers in the text.*

understand /ˌʌndərˈstænd/ v. ★★★ entender *Do you understand the question?*

unemployment /ˌʌnɪmˈplɔɪmənt/ n. desemprego *Unemployment is a big problem in our country.*

until /ənˈtɪl/ conj. prep. ★★★ até *I will stay here until you fall sleep.*

updated /ʌpˈdeɪtd/ adj. atualizado *Our software is continually updated and improved.*

upheaval /ʌpˈhiv(ə)l/ n. irrompimento, reviravolta *These upheavals make her life seem like a soap opera.*

upload /ˈʌpˌloʊd/ v. enviar arquivos *I like to upload photos to my blog.*

used to /ˈjust tu/ modal ★★★ costumava *Leo and Annie used to have lunch together every day.*

usually /ˈjuʒuəli/ adv. ★★★ geralmente *My brother usually washes his car at home.*

V

value /ˈvælju/ n. ★★★ valor *You can't put a value on a human life.*

vegetable /ˈvedʒ(ə)təb(ə)l/ n. ★★★ vegetal *Lettuce is a common vegetable in salads.* **vegetarian** vegetariano

village /ˈvɪlɪdʒ/ n. ★★★ vilarejo *They live in a village near the capital.*

voice /vɔɪs/ n. ★★★ voz *I heard his voice in the corridor.*

vulnerability /ˌvʌln(ə)rəˈbɪləti/ n. vulnerabilidade *Due to the vulnerability of certain groups in our society, the government must help.*

W

waist /weɪst/ n. ★★ cintura *Marie is wearing a wide black leather belt around her waist.*

waiter /ˈweɪtər/ n. ★ garçom *My brother is a waiter in a steak house.*

waitress /ˈweɪtrəs/ n. ★ garçonete *She works as a waitress in the evenings.*

walk /wɔk/ v. ★★★ andar *He walks to work every day.*

want /wɑnt/ v. ★★★ querer *I want to travel to China.*

war /wɔr/ n. ★★★ guerra *World War II ended in 1945.*

was /wɑz/ v. past of be *Ivan was my teacher in the 1990s.*

wash /wɑʃ/ v. ★★★ lavar *Wash the dishes, please.*

watch /wɑtʃ/ v. ★★★ ver, assistir *Dorothy and Ron watch TV only on the weekends.*

wavy /ˈweɪvi/ adj. ondulado *Carina has brown wavy hair.*

way /weɪ/ n. ★★★ caminho, via *This way is shorter than on the main road.*

wear /wer/ v. ★★★ vestir *These teenagers wear uniforms to go to school.*

weather /ˈweðər/ n. ★★★ tempo, clima *The weather is good today, really sunny.*

wedding /ˈwedɪŋ/ n. ★★★ (cerimônia de) casamento *Today is my best friend's wedding.*

weight /weɪt/ n. ★★★ peso *We use kilos and grams as a measure of weight.*

weightlifting /ˈweɪtˌlɪftɪŋ/ n. levantamento de peso *Weightlifting is an Olympic sport.*

well /wel/ adv. ★★★ bem *Charlene speaks Italian very well.*

were /wɜr/ v. past of be *We were friends in the early 1980s.*

what /wɑt/ adv. det. predet. inter. pron. ★★★ o que *What is your name?*

wheel /wil/ n. roda *Lucas is cleaning the wheels of his skate board.*

when /wen/ adv. conj. ★★★ quando *When is your birthday?*

where /wer/ adv. ★★★ onde *Where do you live?*

while /waɪl/ conj. ★★★ enquanto *Listen to this song while I have a shower.*

white /waɪt/ n. ★★★ branco *White is the color of the clouds.*

who /hu/ pron. ★★ quem *Who is your favorite singer?*

why /waɪ/ adv. ★★★ por que *Why do dogs bark?*

wide /waɪd/ adj. ★★★ amplo *This is a wide road.*

widely /ˈwaɪdli/ adj. ★★★ amplamente *Organic foods are now much more widely available.*

wild /waɪld/ adj. ★★★ selvagem *This trait is common to both domestic and wild dogs.*

winner /ˈwɪnər/ n. ★★★ vencedor *Jake is the winner of the math competition.*

wireless /ˈwaɪrləs/ adj. conexão sem fio *We use wireless connection here.*

wish /wɪʃ/ v. ★★★ desejar *I wish you a Merry Christmas and a Happy New Year.*

with /wɪθ/ prep. ★★★ com *I live with my mom and my sister.*

without /wɪðˈaʊt/ adv. prep. ★★★ sem *Do not leave without your jacket, it's raining.*

woman /ˈwʊmən/ n. ★★★ mulher *Alice is a woman's name.*

word /wɜrd/ n. ★★★ palavra *I is a very short word.*

work /wɜrk/ v. ★★★ trabalhar *Flight attendants can work up to 18 hours a day.*

world /wɜrld/ n. ★★★ mundo *There are an endless number of living creatures in our world.*

worldwide /ˈwɜrldˌwaɪd/ adj. ★ global *Internet is used worldwide.*

worried /ˈwʌrid/ adj. ★★★ preocupado *Barbra is worried about her science test.*

worse /wɜrs/ adj. ★★★ pior *Cats are worse guardians than dogs.*

would /wʊd/ modal ★★★ gostaria *I would like a glass of water.*

wrap /ræp/ v. ★★ enrolar, embrulhar *Please wrap the present with a nice paper.*

wrestler /ˈreslər/ n. lutador *Anderson Silva is a famous Brazilian wrestler.*

wrestling /ˈres(ə)lɪŋ/ n. luta livre esportiva *Wrestling is a popular sport in Brazil.*

write /raɪt/ v. ★★★ escrever *I always write emails to my friends.*

Y

year /jɪr/ n. ★★★ ano *This is the year 2014.*

yesterday /ˈjestərˌdeɪ/ adv. ★★★ ontem *Yesterday was my sister's birthday.*

yet /jet/ adv. conj. ★★★ ainda *I can't leave the hospital yet – the doctor says maybe tomorrow.*

young /jʌŋ/ adj. ★★★ jovem *My cousin is really young; he is 7 years old.*

Z

zoo /zu/ n. ★ zoológico *This zoo has more than 20 species.*

Minidictionary 163

Website references

Page 15 **AmeliaBurton.com.au** <www.ameliaburton.com.au/2008/08/olympic-body-shapes-what-body-type-are-you-take-the-body-type-test.html>. Acessed August 2011.

Page 56 **KCLibrary.Lonestar.edu** <http://kclibrary.lonestar.edu/decade90.html>. Accessed January 2012.

Wikipedia.org <http://en.wikipedia.org/wiki/1990s>. Accessed January 2012.

Wikipedia.org <http://en.wikipedia.org/wiki/Dolly_%28sheep%29>. Accessed January 2012.

CDN.com <http://www.blogcdn.com/lifestyle.aol.co.uk/media/2010/05/rachel.jpg>. Accessed April 2012.

Page 72 **BodyBuilding.com** <www.bodybuilding.com/fun/becker3.htm>. Accessed April 2012.

ABCya.com <http://www.abcya.com/skeletal_system.htm>. Accessed April 2012.

DailyInfographic.com <http://dailyinfographic.com>. Acessed October 2011.

Accent.gmu.edu <http://accent.gmu.edu/browse_atlas.php>. Accessed April 2012.

Page 73 **OldComputer.net** <oldcomputers.net/oldads/old-computer-ads.html>. Accessed April 2012.

Durso.org <www.durso.org/ynib/>. Accessed April 2012.

Fact Monster.com <http://www.factmonster.com/>. Accessed April 2012.

Page 83 **Wikipedia.org** <http://en.wikipedia.org/wiki/Guaran%C3%AD_people>. Accessed April 2012.

Page 94 **BusinessBalls.com** <http://www.businessballs.com/eq.htm>. Acessed April 2012.

Page 102 **HowToTrainYourDragon.com** <www.howtotrainyourdragon.com>. Accessed April 2012.

Page 108 **RaçaBrasil.uol.com.br** <racabrasil.uol.com.br>. Accessed April 2012.

Africanidades.com <http://www.africaeafricanidades.com/documentos/13052011-11.pdf>. Accessed April 2012.

Page 109 **Wikipedia.org** <http://pt.wikipedia.org/wiki/Stokely_Carmichael>. Accessed January 2012.

Page 117 **Management.about.com** <http://management.about.com/od/communication/ht/PublicSpeaking6.htm>. Accessed April 2012.

Page 132 **ITunes.apple.com** <http://itunes.apple.com/au/album/id324917040>. Accessed April 2012.

Page 136 **Quizilla.Teennick.com** <http://quizilla.teennick.com/hubs/trivia-quizzes>. Accessed April 2012.

Etymonline.com <http://www.etymonline.com/>. Accessed April 2012.

Imdb.com <http://www.imdb.com/title/tt0103352/>. Accessed April 2012.

Page 137 **YouTube.com.br** <www.youtube.com.br>. Accessed April 2012.

GQ.com <http://www.gq.com/style>. Accessed April 2012.

Polyvore.com <http://www.polyvore.com/>. Accessed April 2012.

AfroPop.org <http://www.afropop.org/radio/streams.php>. Accessed April 2012.

TravelBlog.org <www.travelblog.org/World/flags.html>. Accessed April 2012.

Sites

Bibliography

BAKHTIN, M.; VOLOCHINOV, V. N. *Marxismo e filosofia da linguagem*. 11. ed. São Paulo: Hucitec, 2004.

BAWARSHI, A.; DEVITT, A.; REIFF, M. J. *Scenes of Writing: Strategies for Composing with Genres*. New York: Pearson Longman, 2004.

BAZERMAN, C. *Gêneros textuais, tipificação e interação*. São Paulo: Cortez, 2005.

BRASIL. Secretaria de Educação Fundamental. *Parâmetros curriculares nacionais: terceiro e quarto ciclos do Ensino Fundamental: língua estrangeira moderna*. Brasília: MEC, 1998.

BROWN, H. D. Teaching by Principles: *An Interactive Approach to Language Pedagogy*. New York: Pearson, 2001.

COSCARELLI, V. C.; RIBEIRO, A. E. *Letramento digital: aspectos sociais e possibilidades pedagógicas*. Belo Horizonte: Ceale / Autêntica, 2007.

FREIRE, P. *Pedagogia da autonomia: saberes necessários à prática educativa*. São Paulo: Paz e Terra, 1996.

GOWER, R.; PHILLIPS, D.; WALTERS, S. *Teaching Practice. A Handbook for Teachers in Training*. Oxford: Macmillan, 1995.

HARMER, J. *How to Teach English: An Introduction to the Practice of English Language Teaching*. Harlow: Pearson Longman, 2007.

HERNANDEZ, F.; VENTURA, M. *Organização do Currículo por Projetos de Trabalho. O Conhecimento e um Caleidoscópio*. Porto Alegre: Artmed, 1998

JOHNSON, K.; MORROW, K. *Communication in the Classroom*. Harlow: Pearson, 1990.

KLEIMAN, A. B.; MORAES, S. E. *Leitura e interdisciplinaridade: tecendo redes nos projetos da escola*. Campinas: Mercado de Letras, 1999.

KRESS, Gunther. *Reading Images: Multimodality, Representation and New Media*. Disponível em: <www.knowledgepresentation.org/BuildingTheFuture/Kress2/Kress2.html>. Acesso em: 12 dez. 2006.

MEHISTO, P.; MARSH, D.; FRIGOLS, M. J. *Uncovering CLIL: Content and Language Integrated Learning in Bilingual and Multilingual Education*. Oxford: Macmillan, 2008.

MEURER, J. L.; BONINI, A.; MOTTA-ROTH, D. (Org.). *Gêneros: teorias, métodos, debates*. São Paulo: Parábola Editorial, 2005.

NUNAN, D. *Task-Based Language Teaching*. Cambridge: CUP, 2004.

RAJAGOPALAN, K. *Por uma linguística crítica: linguagem, identidade e a questão ética*. São Paulo: Parábola Editorial, 2003.

SCHNEUWLY, B.; DOLZ, J.; HALLER, S. *Gêneros orais e escritos na escola*. Trad. e org. ROJO, R. H. R.; CORDEIRO, G. S. Campinas: Mercado de Letras, 2004.

SCRIVENER, J. *Learning Teaching*. Oxford: Macmillan, 2004.

SIGNORINI, I.; CAVALCANTI, M. C. (Org.). *Linguística aplicada e transdisciplinaridade*. Campinas: Mercado de Letras, 2004.

TANNER, R.; GREEN C. *Tasks for Teacher Education: A Reference Approach Coursebook*. Harlow: Longman, 1998.

THORNBURY, S.; SLADE, D. *Conversation: From Description to Pedagogy*. Cambridge: CUP, 2006.

UR, P. *A Course in Language Teaching: Practice and theory*. Cambridge: CUP, 2001.

When and how to use your DVD-ROM

Multimedia Content 1 – Converting measurements	
When to use	Before *Listening*, page 17 (Unit 1)
Content	Measurement converter.
Purpose	To understand the differences between the American and the metric system.
What to do	Choose between height and weight. Then type your data and see what the equivalent would be in the American measurement system.
Tips	Memorize your measurements in the American system. That will help you have a better understanding next time you hear or read some of these measures.

Multimedia Content 2 – How are pimples formed?	
When to use	Before *Speaking*, page 29 (Unit 2)
Content	Infographics about pimples
Purpose	To show how pimples are formed.
What to do	Read the instructions and understand the formation process of a pimple.
Tips	"*Pimples*" are also called "zits" or "spots".

Multimedia Content 3 – Holidays and celebrations: Valentine's Day	
When to use	After *Writing*, page 35 (Unit 2)
Content	Infographics about Valentine's Day
Purpose	To talk about the origin of Valentine's Day and some trivia about this holiday.
What to do	Read the information carefully. Before looking in a dictionary, try to understand the meanings of the new word by observing the pictures and other words in the sentence.
Tips	After reading the information, try to learn more about the facts that surprised you most.

Multimedia Content 4 – Technology icon	
When to use	Before *Grammar*, page 46 (Unit 3)
Content	Games with icons related to technology
Purpose	To test your knowledge about icons related to technology.
What to do	Relate the icons to the images they represent.
Tips	Think of other icons you see on a daily basis. Would you be able to reproduce them?

Multimedia Content 5 – A technology timeline	
When to use	After *Grammar*, page 48 (Unit 3)
Content	Infographics with a timeline about technology
Purpose	To indicate on a timeline when some technologies were developed.
What to do	Compare your expectations about the time when you think some technologies appeared to the dates when they were actually developed.
Tips	Compare the year when some of these technologies appeared to when they started being part of people's daily lives. Talk to your parents about this.

Multimedia Content 6 – Quiz: historical events	
When to use	After activity 3, page 59 (Unit 4)
Content	*Quiz* about historical events throughout the decades
Purpose	To test your knowledge about when some historical events happened.
What to do	Answer the questions and test your general knowledge.
Tips	An event is never isolated. We can learn a lot by analyzing its causes and consequences. That helps us understand human beings better, try new ways to solve problems, and avoid repeating the same mistakes from the past.

Multimedia Content 7 – The legend of the Vitória Régia	
When to use	After *Grammar*, page 83 (Unit 5)
Content	*Video about a Brazilian indigenous legend*
Purpose	To tell the Brazilian indigenous legend of Victoria Regia.
What to do	Watch the video carefully. At the end, try to retell the legend in your own words. Watch the video once again and check how close to the original you got.
Tips	Pay attention to key words in each scene, especially verbs and nouns in each sentence.

Multimedia Content 8 – Occupations	
When to use	After working on page 93 (Unit 6)
Content	Vocabulary about occupations
Purpose	To practice vocabulary related to occupations.
What to do	Type letters which you believe to be part of the hidden word. For each correct word, an image will appear. Observe the parts of the images, remember what you have learned in class, and find out what the hidden words are.
Tips	When you memorize new words, try to associate the images not only with the sounds, but also with the feelings you associate with the words. For example, when you think of "cook", visualize the image of a cook, "listen in your mind" to the sound of the word, and try to remember the smell of some food. When we associate a word in this way, this increases our chances to remember the word in the future.

Multimedia Content 9 – Telephone conversations	
When to use	After working on page 111 (Unit 7)
Content	Game about articles of clothing
Purpose	To practice the vocabulary studied in complete sentences.
What to do	Look at the pictures and click the alternative that describes what the person is wearing.
Tips	Before reading the alternatives, try to describe what the person in the picture is wearing. In this way, it will be much easier to know what the correct alternative is.

Multimedia Content 10 – Some countries in the world	
When to use	After activity 1, page 123 (Unit 8)
Content	Interactive game about the location of countries mentioned in *Crossroads*.
Purpose	To teach the location of the countries mentioned, in addition to providing extra information about each one of them.
What to do	Click on the countries' flags and see where the countries are located. Read the extra information about each one of them.
Tips	Before clicking on the flags, activate your knowledge and try to predict where the countries are located.

Capa: **Getty Images:** Sarun Laowong/Getty Images (canoas) Marla Rutherford/ Getty Images (safari) Fred Paul/GettyImages (garota)

© **DreamWorks Animation SKG.:** 102 (poster)

© **Sony Corporation:** 45

ABR: Antonio Cruz 131 (Joaquim Barbosa)

Agência O Globo: Osmar Gallo 70 (1g)

Arcady: 72, 73, 136, 137 (placa)

Arquivo pessoal da autora: 71 (4, 3 primeiras), 128 (caneca)

Autorização de reprodução de Sandra Natalini: 71 (4, última)

Autorização de reprodução Jorge Barreto: 132 (Banda Black Rio)

Autorização de reprodução de Adora Svitak: 92

Autorização de reprodução de Harisim Tiaz Khan: 92

Autorização de reprodução de Harisim Marc-Yu: 92

Autorização de reprodução de Harisim Marko Calasan: 92

Capa DVD Vitus: 90

Conteudo Expresso: 111 (2b, 2c)

Editora Abril: José Antonio 70 (1c)

Folhapress: Daniel Marenco 131 (Hélio de la Peña), Jarbas Oliveira 131 (Milton Santos), Jorge Araújo 108 (Zezé Mota), Lula Marques 70 (1h), Folhapress 108 (Toni Tornado), 111 (2a)

Gabriella Fabbri: 133

Getty Images: AFP 131 (Benedita da Silva), 134 (3e), FilmMagic 131 (Alexandre Pires), Gamma Rapho 131 (Margareth Menezes), Image Source 89, Jeff Greenberg 110 (homem de óculos), Jim Steinfeldt- 70 (1d), Jupiterimages 119, Karan Kapoor 12 (turma), LatinContent 131 (Anderson Silva), LatinContent 131 (Marina Silva), LatinContent 131 (Paula Lima), NBA Photos 110 (jogador), Plush Studios 88, Rahav Segev WireImage 62, Romilly Lockyer 106, Thomas Busk 20 (1d), Getty Images 40 (aula), 40 (equilíbrio), 40 (twister), 42 (aspirador esquerda), 42 (geladeira esquerda), 43 (telefone esquerda), 57 (Jennifer Aniston), 83 (índios), 104 (direita), 105 (apresentadores), 105 (mulher), 108 (Carmichael), 108 (casal), 113 (James Brown), 114 (1d), 134 (3c), 134 (3d), 135 (4-centro), 135 (4-direita), 135 (4-esquerda)

Globo: 108 (Tim Maia)

Jupiterimages: 47 (2b)

Latinstock: Corbis-Corbis 70 (1e)

Memo Pad executado por **Karen Tiemy Ohara:** 128 (memo pad)

Menno Equipamentos para Escritório Ltda: 49 (3f)

SambaPhoto: Almir Bindilatti 85

Shutterstock: a-poselenov 75 (3e), AbleStock 121 (celofane), AbleStockcom 75 (3c), AFH 110 (mulher de laranja), Ahmed Aboul-Seoud 69 (bolsa), Albo003 48 (disquete), Alexander Chaikin 58 (exército), Alexander Ishchenko 58 (rios), Alexander Raths 19 (atleta), 19 (senhora), Alexandr Makarov 121 (1c), Alexey Stiop 121 (papel de presente), Alila Sao Mai 39 (6), anarhist 50 (2b), Andrea Chu 93 (2a), Andrei Marincas 46 (errey), Andrew Chin 123 (bandeira da índia), Anton Novik 46 (roteador), AnutkaT 121 (cartolina), art&design 67 (3), Artisticco 37, Asparuh 144 (3-direita), Baloncici 144 (3-esquerda), Bobb Klissourski 34, Bruno Passigatti 50 (2c), CABO 122 (scrapbook), Calek 60 (bebê), Carsten Medom Madsen 75 (3d), Cheryl Casey 19 (dentista), ChipPix 142 (3b), Chyiacat 28 (sutiã), claires 17 (3e), Claudia Naerdemann 33 (menino com aros), Computer Earth 69 (banco), corepics 138 (2a), cosma 28 (pés), Couperfield 60 (antes e depois), Creatista 28 (menino), Dariusz Kantorski 144 (1), Darko Zeljkovic 75 (d), Dawid Konopka 75 (c), Dawn Hudson 98 (tatu), dean bertoncelj 112 (meninas), Denis and Yulia Pogostins 121 (1g), design56 120 (pote), didden 50 (2f), Diego Barbieri 16 (homem), digitalconsumator 39 (4a), Dirk Ercken 114 (1b), djem 40 (dardos), Dmitriy Shironosov 64 (ginástica), ejwhite 79 (calcanhar), ekler 121 (bandeira da China), elena moiseeva 120 (purpurina), Elena Ray 61 (carro), Elzbieta Sekowska 61 (menina e homem), 61 (moto), 142 (3c), EMJAY SMITH 15 (homem de vermelho), Entertainment Press 101 (2d), Eric Isselée 56, 57, ermess 114 (1a), Featureflash 101 (2e), Fedorov Oleksiy 39 (4c), Fotofermer

79 (lacre), fred goldstein 82 (casal), Fred Kamphues 100 (2c), G. Campbell 100 (minotauro), Gelpi 121 (1b), Gemenacom 67 (1a), Georgios Kollidas 49 (3d), Gina Sanders 61 (olhando álbum), Goodluz 47 (2d), Goygel-Sokol Dmitry 117, Hannah Eckman 48 (controle remoto), Herbert Kratky 14 (1c), HGalina 44 (balança), Hilch 46 (bateria vermelha), Howard Sandler 40 (tabuleiro), hurricane 44 (vitrola), Iev dolgachov 32 (menina), Igor Bulgarin 96, igor kisselev 67 (1b), Igor Sokolov 120 (cola quente), ilker canikligil 48 (video game), iofoto 58 (trânsito), iQoncept 46 (hodômetro), 58 (crianças), 104 (dados), iStockphoto 114 (1f), Jaimie Duplass 75 (3a), jakelv7500 129 (dragão, flores, borboleta, castelo, cartão vermelho), James Steidl 49 (3c), James Steidl 60 (hospital), jiri jura 120 (boneco), jmatzick 122 (pinhata), John T Takai 36, Jsatt83 15 (homem preto e branco), Juice Team 17 (loira), Julia Zakharova 69 (jeans), Julija Sapic 121 (jornal), Kacso Sandor 47 (2e), Kelly Richardson 74 (cachorro branco), kentoh 58 (palavras), Khoroshunova Olga 138 (mergulhador), Kitch Bain 121 (1d), Kristin Smith 60 (penteado), Kurhan 60 (dentes), l i g h t p o e t 17 (olho), Lana Langlois 121 (colar), Lasse Kristensen 58 (desempregado), Linda Muir 28 (absorvente), liquidlibrary 121 (menino), Lisa F. Young 52 (alunos), LVV 121 (papel laminado), Malgorzata Kistryn 129 (papai noel), mauricio avramow 33 (menino de branco), Meawpong 40 (caderno), Melissa King 75 (3b), Michael Roeder 123 (bandeira da França), michaeljung 121 (casal), 134 (1), Monkey Business Images 60 (família), 75 (3f), Monkik 18 (esqueleto), Morten Normann Almeland 50 (2d), mypockik 121 (papel colorido), Natalia Siverina 49 (3e), Nattika 120 (fitas), New Image 121 (pintar), Nicholas Rjabow 14 (1f), Noam Armonn 47 (2c), Norman Pogson 93 (2j), nulinukas 121 (caixa), Oleg Senkov 83 (livros), Olga Miltsova 120 (cola), Olga Popova 71 (rádio), ostill 17 (grisalho), OtnaYdur 126 (1-direita), PashOK 17 (3c), Patalakha Serg 69 (espada), Paul Orr copy 54, Pavel Gaja 51 (matrix), Peter albreksten 33 (menino de preto), Petro Feketa 64 (maquiagem), photomak 28 (desodorante), PhotoNAN 100 (labirinto), PhotoStock10 14 (1b), pixinity 108 (mulher), Poulsons Photography 31, 75 (costas), POYSTUDIO 44 (auto-falante), R. Gino Santa Maria 123 (bandeira da rússia), Ragnarock 44 (disco), ratselmeister 51 (código binário), restyler 44 (pilha), Rikard Stadler 33 (menino de azul), Robert Jakatics 121 (papel crepon), Rocket400 Studio 98 (controle de video game), Ron Kacmarcik 84, Ronald Sumners 29, 148 (1), Route66 123 (bandeira da Grécia, da Itália, dos EUA, do Japão e da Inglaterra), rudall30 15 (homem de verde), runzelkorn 74 (mecânicos), Rustam Shigapov 44 (cabo de carro), s_bukley 100 (2b), S.john 114 (1c), Serhiy Kyrychenko 17 (ruiva), shooarts 121 (papel kraft), spillikin 121 (1e), Sportgraphic 14 (1a ciclismo), 14 (1g), 16 (salto), Stefan Schurr 16 (ciclismo), stephan kerkhofs 138 (4 fotos navio submerso), Stephen Bonk 71 (boia), StockLite 47 (2f), Stocksnapper 144 (2), Supertrooper 121 (1a), Supri Suharjoto 43 (telefone direita), Suzanne Tucker 28 (espinha), 39 (4b), Tamara Kulikova 33 (menino de verde), 114 (1g), tatiana sayig 17 (afro), TerraceStudio 129 (árvores), Tinga 135 (camisetas), titelio 50 (1), turtix 114 (1e), Ungor 50 (2a), Upadhyay 74 (ovos), Vaclav Volrab 91, val lawless 127 (amarelo), 127 (marrom), 127 (vermelho), Valeria73 97 (show), Valua Vitaly 28 (barbear), Vasca 142 (3a), Vasyl Helevachuk 50 (2e), vipflash 100 (2a), Volodymyr Krasyuk 44 (cabo), waihoo 127 (gato laranja), 127 (gato preto), wavebreakmedia ltd 47 (2a), withGod 99, Wolfgang Kruck 121 (1f), xalanx 139 (2b), Xico Putini 71 (planta), Yuri Arcurs 42 (geladeira direita), Zakowski cartooniz_com 58 (primeiros socorros), Zoltan Pataki 48 (3a), Zoran Karapancev 101 (2f), Shutterstock 7 (televisão), 14 (1a natação), 14 (1e), 16 (peso), 17 (3b), 22 (cavalo), 26, 28 (jeans), 30, 35 (ícone digital), 40 (cartas), 44 (firra cassete), 48 (3b), 58 (tempo), 74 (cachorro preto), 93 (2e), 93 (2h), 93 (2i), 93 (ícone digital), 95, 102 (fundo), 108 (homem), 150 (Justin Bieber), 72, 73, 136, 137 (carinha feliz), 72, 73, 136, 137 (carinha triste)

Thinkstock: BananaStock 42 (aspirador direita), Brand X Pictures 16 (corredor), Comstock 14 (1d), 14 (1h), 67 (1e), 120 (2), 150 (meninas), Creatas 143, David Hiller 93 (2c), Digital Vision 112 (meninos), Hemera 14 (1a corrida), 16 (sumô), 46 (antena de sinal), Hemera Technologies 15 (homem de amarelo), 33 (menino com malabares), iStockphoto 8 (máquina), 16 (cavalo), 17 (3f), 20 (1b), 20 (1c), 24 (menina no muro), 32 (menino), 67 (1d), 93 (2b), 93 (3-homem), 93 (3-mulher), 98 (flor), 105 (voto), 113 (vinil), 121 (folhas de sulfite), 126 (1-esquerda), Jupiterimages 17 (3a), 93 (2d), liquidlibrary 125, Photodisc 17 (3d), 20 (1a), PhotoObjects_net 110 (menino), Photos_com 110 (homem no escritório), 115 (menina), Photoscom 67 (1c), Stockbyte 93 (2f), 93 (2g), 110 (mulher de rosa), Wavebreak Medi 52 (listening), Thinkstock 31 (frente)

Wikipedia: Cavernosa 134 (3b), EuclidC 104 (esquerda), Henry Akorsu 134 (3a), Juang 70 (1f), Metro-Goldwyn-Mayer Inc 70 (1b), NASA Alan L. Bean 70 (1a), Ravi Misra 40 (jogo), S. A. Sisson Azevedo 115 (homem), Yugeshp 92, Wikipedia 82 (estátua), 131 (José do Patrocínio)

Macmillan Dictionary: usado como referência na produção do *Minidictionary*.

Todos os direitos reservados. Nenhuma parte desta publicação pode ser reproduzida, estocada por qualquer sistema ou transmitida por quaisquer meios ou formas existentes ou que venham a ser criados, sem prévia permissão por escrito da Editora.

Este material contém links para sites de terceiros. Não controlamos ou nos responsabilizamos pelos conteúdos destes sites. Favor usar de cautela ao acessá-los.

Todos os esforços foram feitos no sentido de encontrar os detentores dos direitos das obras protegidas por copyright. Caso tenha havido alguma omissão involuntária, os editores terão o maior prazer em corrigi-la na primeira oportunidade.

O material de publicidade e propaganda reproduzido nesta obra está sendo utilizado única e exclusivamente para fins didáticos, não representando qualquer tipo de recomendação de produtos ou empresas por parte dos autores e da editora.

Há reproduções de artigos de revistas ou jornais em que são mencionadas pessoas reais. Seus nomes foram mantidos, porém, suas fotos foram substituídas para preservar suas imagens.

As fotos / imagens que não constam desta relação têm seus créditos na página onde aparecem em razão de exigências contratuais.